STOLEN

LOVE AND LOSS IN THE TIME OF COVID-19

ELIZABETH JAEGER

Attention schools and businesses: for discounted copies on large orders, please contact the publisher directly.

For information contact:
Unsolicited Press
Portland, Oregon
www.unsolicitedpress.com
orders@unsolicitedpress.com
619-354-8005

Cover Design: Kathryn Gerhardt
Editor: Summer Stewart

ISBN: 978-1-963115-49-9

To Gary Alan Jaeger III

May you always remember your grandfather's love

&

In Loving Memory of

Gary Alan Jaeger Sr.

STOLEN

INTRODUCTION

On Thursday, March 12, 2020, my son came home from fourth grade with a Chromebook. A week prior, I had a meeting at work (at the time, I was a writing professor at Fairleigh Dickinson University), and my supervisor instructed each of us to devise a plan in case the coronavirus caused the world to shut down. My colleagues and I all thought it was extreme, a worst-case scenario exercise, not something we would ever have to implement. Then I saw the Chromebook my son ditched against the living room wall upon entering the condo, and the room slowly started to swirl. I had to sit down. I don't believe in premonitions, but if I did, I'd point to that moment and insist that's when I knew that the world was about to change. Not just the collective world. My world. My life. Everything.

The following day, my son had no school. It was a scheduled day off, not pandemic-related. But by Friday night, his Cub Scout meeting was canceled, as was the potluck event my son's Taekwondo instructor had planned for Pi Day. My spouse also received word that the high school at which she taught math would go remote starting Monday. But it was not just our personal activities and jobs that were shutting down. Disney closed its parks. The NBA put the season on hold. This was serious, not just an exercise in caution.

At first, my son's school told the parents that lessons would be remote until the end of spring break—only a few weeks away. March 16th was his first day of remote learning, and it was miserable for all of us—my son, my spouse, and myself. We were living in a tiny condo. The wi-fi connection in the living room was good, but in my son's room it was weak and unreliable. Since my spouse needed to teach online, she set up an office in the living room. So that my son and I wouldn't interfere with her classes, she banished us to his small room. It held his loft bed, a narrow bookcase, and a desk. There was not room for much else. Needless to say, just an hour into the school day, we were cranky and screaming at each other.

That evening, on a complete whim, after we had eaten dinner and I had read with my son, I set up a WordPress website. Days earlier, my son told me that he wanted to collaborate with me on a writing project. He was thinking fiction, but this seemed a perfect opportunity to encourage him to write personal narratives.

For me, writing has always been an escape, a way to vent my feelings. I thought my son and I could keep a Pandemic Diary. Each day, we'd write our own separate entries and use the space to complain about everything that pissed us off: boring assignments, having to be quiet while my spouse was teaching, being trapped in a place too small to even pace, the loud landscaping equipment outside, and not being able to go to Taekwondo. When I presented the idea to my son, I emphasized the fact that I intended it to be fun, that I wouldn't monitor his words or in any way tell him what he could or couldn't write about. He can be very funny when he is frustrated or furious, and I thought a written record of his thoughts during the pandemic might be fun to look back on in the future. A friend of mine often says that adversity makes for good writing. That the more miserable you are in the moment, the better the story you will have to tell. I just didn't realize at the time the degree of adversity that we would face or how miserable we'd become. As for myself, I had hoped to produce a record that would make me laugh when the pandemic ended. Instead, I wrote a story saturated with tears.

The first week is silly, whiny, and fairly repetitious. My son and I bitched about things that, in retrospect, were not even important. But on Day 8, my premonition came true. My father got sick. Very sick. Since I had already been writing the blog for fun, I didn't stop. Instead, I shifted my focus. My blogging became a way for me to update family and friends on Dad's condition. And when that quickly became overwhelming and depressing, I added memories of happy times spent with Dad. Since my initial audience was people who knew me—some better than others—my tone was friendly and familiar. When I went back to compile the first sixty days into a manuscript, I decided to keep the same tone. To change it would have altered more than just my narrative voice. And by the end, I suspect you, too, will know me very well. I kept no secrets and made no effort to hide my pain and vulnerability. As for my son, once his beloved grandfather got sick, he refused to write. Getting him to do anything became a challenge. Since he only wrote a few entries, I opted not to include them here.

Throughout my daily reflections, you will see me not only as a daughter but as a mother, a teacher, and an individual. Grief is complex, and it permeated every aspect of my family's life. What follows is a deeply personal account, but many of my experiences are not unique to me. COVID affected everyone. The pandemic altered all of our lives. And death is ubiquitous. I may have been writing about my father and my life in New York City when it was the epicenter of the virus, but my words speak to issues and experiences far greater than myself.

DAY 1

MARCH 16, 2020

I hate technology. It is beyond me. I have a computer, and I can use it for basic functions like Word and accessing the internet. But the less I have to use it, the happier I am. Therefore, this whole switch to online teaching and learning has me functioning on the verge of a panic attack. Don't get me wrong. I support all the government shutdowns. But if I am going to live in isolation, my preference would be a remote village in the middle of nowhere. Nepal, perhaps. Somewhere deep in the Himalayan Mountains. I would be happiest without modern technology. Yes, I would even venture deeper into the void—no running water, no electricity. Give me pens and paper, a stack of novels, and I would be content. But trying to navigate my way through apps and links and videos—it has only been a day, and I have a headache.

This morning was nothing short of chaotic. Ten minutes after breakfast, my son, my spouse, and I were all yelling at each other. I blame technology. Give me workbooks and textbooks and I could happily teach my son at home indefinitely. Perhaps here would be a good place to point out that I am a teacher certified in English, social studies, and elementary education. My spouse is a certified math teacher. Give us the books, and we are good to go. But my son's school does not use books, not like I used to when I was a kid, so the work is being posted on Google Classroom. Of course, my son forgot his log-in information, and so we started the morning unable to access his math work. He complained about writing. He complained about reading. He complained about everything.

And having to sort through the material online set off my very short fuse.

While he proceeded to have a breakdown, I had to send emails to my own classes. I currently work as an adjunct professor teaching college writing. I am glad it is writing and not something completely dependent on lectures and discussions. At least I can easily comment on drafts from afar so that students can revise their work. But my boss emailed me: she wants updated plans indicating how I will implement technology to make learning effective. Understandably so. But to do a fabulous job, I would need technological skills, and trying to teach myself new skills while dealing with a temperamental ten-year-old was not happening.

After sending out emails to my students, a few papers trickled in. I tried to comment on them. I didn't get far. I succeeded in reading only three of them before I had to tend to a meltdown. Part of the problem with my son is he views the work he has to complete as "busy work." Some of it is. But what are teachers to do? I get it. They, like me, are also wrestling with this new situation. However, some of the work could be interesting, dare I say even fun. If only he'd give it a chance. The science experiment was hands-on and better than a boring worksheet. But he still grumbled about it.

Throughout the day, I accomplished very little. For someone goal oriented, this was incredibly maddening. I was especially disappointed that I had no time to write. Usually, on days when I don't teach, I try to get at least two hours of writing done. Not today. I suspect that through the duration of this pandemic, my novel, the one I recently started to write, will ground to a halt. I am hoping that once my spouse, son, and I settle into a routine, I will be able to find at least a half hour a day to exercise my creative thoughts.

Maybe it is too much to hope for. Maybe I should focus my energy on staying healthy and keeping my family safe.

DAY 2

MARCH 17, 2020

My parents are home. They touched down yesterday morning. In late February, they headed down south—the far south, Patagonia, to be exact—for a Viking cruise along the tip of South America. Ever since my dad retired, almost ten years ago, they have become world travelers. Every year, they take at least one cruise, sometimes two. This year, they were excited to explore Argentina and Chile, but within a week of them being gone, I started to panic. With the Princess Cruise ship hanging out off the coast of California and people unable to disembark, my anxiety spiked. My parents are not young. They both fall into the vulnerable category. Of all the possible souvenirs they could bring back, I did not want a deadly disease to be one of them.

Toward the end of last week, as the number of coronavirus cases increased world-wide, I started following the news out of Argentina. It did nothing to ease my concerns. While the numbers in Buenos Aires are fewer than those in New York, they are growing. Plus, Argentina, like many countries in Europe, and even the United States, were closing their borders. I sent my dad a message, asking when he was coming home. Sure, he had emailed me that information before he left, but when one is panicking, it's easier to ask a question than it is to search out an answer. It is a good thing I asked because the original information was no longer accurate. The Argentinian government was kicking foreigners out and sending them home. My parents had to cut their trip short, missing out on an extra day in the capital and a day trip to Iguazu Falls.

But the good news was, they were not sick. Yet. They still had to take a long flight home. And the pictures posted on social media regarding the crowds in the airports—due to Trump's bungling of the situation—were frightening. In trying to stop the spread of a deadly virus, crowds are to be avoided. Apparently, that simple fact did not compute for the president. I was up half the night of their flight worried about them, hoping they could run the gauntlet of germs and return safely. As it turned out, they landed shortly after dawn, and the airport was empty. But now the waiting game begins. If they did get infected on the plane, we might not know for a couple of weeks.

Today has not been much better than yesterday. The days still start exactly like my days used to start. I wake up and exercise. My gym is in my garage so I can still lift weights and walk. However, after my work-out, I skip the part of my routine where I would get my son's lunch ready for school. Instead, I jump right in the shower. What follows is one of my favorite parts of the day. My son cuddles up on my lap and reads to me. We started reading in the morning seven years ago when I began teaching him how to read, and I have not wanted to give it up. It may have begun as a way for me to monitor his reading, to see how he was growing as a reader, but now it is simply a way for us to share a good book. Recently, he has wanted to tackle some classics. So, he read me *Tom Sawyer* and *Call of the Wild*. This morning it was *Hound of the Baskervilles*. He loves mysteries so much, I thought it only right that I introduce him to Sherlock Holmes. At roughly six pages a day, it takes a while to read the more grown-up books, but he seems to be enjoying it, and that is all that matters.

Breakfast follows reading. This morning, it was corn bread, and since my parents are back home, they resumed their morning FaceTime call with my son. But the calm did not last long. As soon as my son finished eating, he had to do schoolwork. Chaos ripped through the room. Another round of screaming and crying because he didn't want to do anything "stupid and boring." Luckily, he did settle down more quickly than yesterday.

What really bums me out is that we can no longer go to Taekwondo. It was my one release from the stress of otherwise having my life turned upside down. But last night, by order of Governor Murphy, all gyms in New Jersey—including Taekwondo studios—had to shut their doors. Our instructor is making videos and trying to figure out how to run classes remotely, but unfortunately, that will not work for us. Our condo is tiny, and we have no room to spread out and practice anything. We would go to kick a pad and end up breaking our toe on the banister.

DAY 3

MARCH 18, 2020

When you live with a math teacher, what might seem like a simple question becomes an entire lesson. Last night, while we were watching CNN, my son asked what it means when something increases exponentially. My spouse immediately fell into teacher mode. She asked our son, "Would you rather have $1,000 on the first day of a month, or would you rather I give you a dollar on the first day and then double it each day after that?" Well, as expected, he chose the first option because it sounded better. But as soon as he gave his answer, my spouse whipped out a white board and a dry-erase marker and told him to start calculating. As the numbers grew, his eyes opened wider. On day one, he would get $1. Day two, $2. Day three, $4. But by the time he hit day 11, he would get $1,024. The numbers only continued to grow at a surprising rate. Day fourteen, $8,192. Day twenty-one, $1,048,576. And finally, day thirty would yield $536,870,912. When you add it all up—the money gotten on each day over the course of the month— what had started as a single dollar now amounted to more than a billion dollars. Suddenly, what initially seemed the smarter choice was not nearly as appealing as the alternative. But money is one thing. The question arose because of the virus, and when you look at the numbers—people infected and people dying—multiplying on the television screen, one is not so much awed as frightened. This, we explained to our son, is why we can't go out. Why all our fun activities have been canceled. Why he is learning at home instead of at school. Because we don't want those numbers going up. We don't want his grandparents to get sick.

Even though my son is ten, we still read together before bed. Until he grumbles that he has outgrown it, I will continue the tradition. We had been reading the Narnia books. But after completing *The Horse and His Boy*, my son decided to take a break from Narnia to read some of the fairy tales written by Hans Christian Andersen. Several years ago, his grandparents traveled to Denmark on vacation and bought him a collection of Andersen's stories. Last night, he asked me to read "The Emperor's New Clothes," a fitting story for our current political environment. The connection was not lost on my son. He made several references to Trump and how he could see Trump marching down the street naked, believing that his clothes were invisible. Perhaps a public shaming is what our president needs, but I am not sure it would be effective. He would still find a way to bully the spectators and twist the truth to fit his lie.

Perhaps we are watching too much CNN. Perhaps we are talking too much about the spiking death toll so my son is more aware of the fatalities than he needs to be. Today, for school, he had to log into a "morning meeting." His teacher instructed the students to "Write about a place in the world you would like to visit someday." His response was unlike any of his classmates' responses: "I would probably take turns visiting my grandparents. I would do this because with COVID-19, they may not have so long, so I would want to spend as much time as possible with them."

DAY 4

MARCH 19, 2020

I am living in a dystopian novel. And dystopian novels never end well. Perhaps that explains my sudden apathy—about everything. Of course, each novel is different, so it is impossible to completely predict what life will be like on the other side of this pandemic. But it will not be the same. Life as we knew it is over.

Specifically, things are rapidly changing in education. This need for technology will undoubtedly have far reaching consequences in the classroom. What is new and confusing now, will become the norm. But I wonder, when this is over, will Americans remember how teachers scrambled to learn technology in order to keep their classes running? Will they remember how hard some teachers worked to get lessons to students so they could continue to learn? Or will they only remember that teachers abandoned their posts as daycare workers? That they were no longer free and dependable babysitters? I will be surprised if teachers come out of this better than they went in. Already, teachers are poorly paid in many areas. They struggle to pay rent, put food on the table, and provide their own kids with many of the activities other parents can easily provide for their children. Teachers are babysitters; education is just a byproduct of what they do. And anyone can babysit. As the pandemic worsens, government officials are reinforcing this idea. Schools cannot close because kids will have nowhere to go. Parents with important jobs will not be able to show up to work. Or so it sounds when I listen to Governor Cuomo speak.

Maybe I should stop reading dystopian novels and the news, at least for the moment. It is all too depressing, and it does nothing to improve my mood. Maybe I should limit my reading to rainbows and unicorns.

My son, I believe, is also depressed. And I think it is not just being stuck at home that has him down. He had three big Taekwondo tournaments coming up in the next three weekends. Of course, they have all been canceled. Two of those tournaments would have required a road trip—one to Pittsburgh and the other to Hollis, New Hampshire. And we all love road trips, getting out of this condo, this town. Going somewhere new, exploring different areas of the country. To compound his disappointment, the trip to New Hampshire was supposed to be followed by a family reunion, dinner with relatives I did not even know existed until six months ago.

He worked hard all year, practiced to fine-tune his forms and improve his sparring. He had aspirations of qualifying for districts this spring. And after his last tournament—after placing in forms, weapons, and sparring—he was on the point boards in New Jersey, so it's not like it was a far-fetched dream. It was realistically within his grasp. But now, all that effort and excitement has been rewarded with his Taekwondo studio shutting down. He lost the thing he looks forward to most, the activity that makes him happy and provides him with a sense of self-confidence, a boost to his self-esteem. No wonder he is struggling to get up and push through the day. All that remains of his former life is the schoolwork he never liked, the videos and worksheets that bore him.

Remote learning is not working for either me or my son. I want to pull him out of school and homeschool him. My own plans. My own lessons. No technology. That way I am not wasting time chasing things on the computer. I am not tracking his teacher's comments and following what she's doing. Seriously, I am a writing professor and a certified elementary school teacher. Do you have any idea how frustrating it is for me to watch my son watch videos about something I could teach him? Me working one-on-one with him would be more effective. I understand that teachers are strapped and that they are doing the best they can. And for many kids, that is fantastic. But those kids do not live with a teacher.

DAY 5

MARCH 20, 2020

Back in my former life, the one I was living before I got stuck in this altered reality, we would have been leaving for Pittsburgh today. The plan was to pick up my son from school early, after I had completed teaching my classes, and get on the road by three. With luck, and not much traffic, we would have been there in time to grab a late dinner.

My son has worked hard training these last few months, and we were optimistic that he would do well. But last week, we got the devastating news. The tournament was canceled. We were not surprised. The virus threat rapidly evolved. We went from being distantly concerned about it to suddenly being thrust into a whirlwind of closures and shutdowns, bans on large crowds, and the suspension of all sorts of sporting events. Today, the disappointment is weighing on me like a boulder. It was not just the excitement of watching my son compete that I was looking forward to, it was also the prospect of getting out of New Jersey.

I wish I could still escape. Being stuck at home is torture. Trying to juggle all aspects of my life is impossible. Today, my boss kindly told me I was not putting in enough time or working hard enough, but my son is already grumbling that we do not care about him. That we have discarded him in favor of our own students. So I need to choose, and at the moment, I choose my son. I commented on one student paper, set up a discussion board for each of my classes, and then shut down the computer. I had no idea it had gotten so warm outside. Seventy-four degrees. Spring. Spring during a pandemic. Why couldn't this happen in the winter when it was cold? Anyway, we can't mingle with people or socialize, but we can still leave home, so we jumped on our bikes and headed out for a ride.

It is not until after dinner, when my son and spouse are asleep, that I have a moment of quiet in which to indulge in a glass of wine. If I close my eyes, I can almost pretend that life is normal. Tomorrow is Saturday. No stress. No work. But no Taekwondo—our usual Saturday morning classes—either. However, we will have a family day. Maybe. If the roads do not get shut down and we can escape into the mountains. I have no idea what will greet us at the other end of this pandemic. Life will not be the same. I may or may not have a job. I may or may not be able to move. I may or may not get a break with my writing. But I'll have my family—hopefully—and I'll have my wine. I'll take it!

DAY 6

MARCH 21, 2020

We had to get out. A hike—after a week of being trapped in this jail cell of a condo—a retreat into the woods seemed more than a necessity. If I did not go on a long hike, if I did not feel the fresh air on my skin, I would have died. I needed hope. And getting out seemed the only way to find it. However, the moment we left, it was apparent things were not normal. Usually, when we take a road trip, we wake up early and grab breakfast on the road. On hiking days, we aim to get egg sandwiches. They taste good and they fill us up, ensuring that we make it to lunch without grumbling stomachs. I also get a medium coffee for the road. This morning, we packed dry Cheerios and I made a pot of espresso to pour into a travel mug. We were not taking any chances. The roads were practically deserted. My son asked if he could bring his CDs, and after listening to the news, hearing the latest number of people who have contracted the virus, and more depressing, the rise in deaths, my son handed me an Aerosmith CD.

As the music played, I tried to forget the outside world. I closed my eyes, and the lyrics of the songs carried me back to high school. My best friend, Libby, used to love going to the dances at Molloy High School. It was a Catholic all-boys school at the time, and they would host dances and invite girls from neighboring schools. I went because it was the thing to do. Because Libby went, and I wanted to feel as if I actually fit in somewhere. When "Angel" began to play in the car, I started to sing along, and a blurred image of the dance floor formed in my memory. "Angel" was at the top of the charts all those years ago, so it played all the time. At all the dances.

23

At fourteen—and now I am totally dating myself—I had no idea that it was Aerosmith who sang the song. But it was not only music I was ignorant of back then. I knew, deep down, that something was wrong with me. That I was not normal. That the things that made other girls gossip and laugh held no interest for me. But I went to a Catholic school, and I had strict conservative parents. The term "lesbian" was a bad word, a term reserved for women one did not like. If anyone had told me I was a lesbian, I would have been hurt and insulted. It was something I did not want to be. So, I tried to play the game. Obviously, not very well. I felt uncomfortable about the idea of dating boys, but that was the expectation, so that was what I did. I went to dances and pretended I was like everyone else, and I endured the misery of it so that no one would call me out. No one would make me feel more alone than I already was. If someone had told me back in high school that I would end up married to a woman, I just might have hit them. And yet, here I am.

We went to Monument Mountain Reservation in Great Barrington. Yes, we drove three hours for a day trip. That is how desperate I was—we were. On the trail, my son vacillated between complaining about having to walk—yes, even on a day that we were out and about, away from all things he kvetched about all week, he still complained—and having fun going off to explore and climb all the rocks strewn through the park. He wore the duster jacket my spouse made him two years ago for Halloween when he dressed as Mad-Eye Moody, and he brought the heavy walking stick that went with the costume. On his head, he wore his aviator hat, which, in an odd sort of way, went with the jacket. His attire drew looks from others on the trail, and two people complimented his jacket. Jammed into his belt was the cap gun he got for Christmas. At times, he would stop, climb up onto a big boulder, sit down, and fire. The smell of caps permeated the air.

It was not until we reached the end of the trail that I noticed the COVID-19 warning that was posted, telling people that trails might be crowded and we should keep our distance from each other. The trail wasn't too crowded, and for the most part, people stayed far away from each other, but the trails can't possibly stay open. It would be irresponsible. Today, it was only forty degrees. When the weather warms, people will swarm the state and local parks. They will become like the beaches down in Florida during spring break. The only way to keep people away is to shut them down, the way the government has shut down bars, and restaurants, and movie theaters.

Along with Governor Cuomo shutting down New York, our governor, Murphy, is shutting down New Jersey. As of eight o'clock tonight, we will be virtual prisoners in our homes. Only stores carrying essential goods will be allowed to open. Grocery stores are a given. As are pharmacies. But my spouse's question of the day was, "Are liquor stores considered essential?" It turns out they are. We will be able to keep a constant supply of wine to get us through this shelter-in-place, which could go on for months—until mid-summer. So much for our Disney and Great Lakes vacations. I suppose there is always next year.

"Can we watch *Contagion*," my son asked when we got home.

"Absolutely not," I answered, unwilling to even entertain the idea. Two weeks ago, we made the poor parenting decision to watch *Outbreak*. Big mistake. All through the movie, my son kept asking if it was fiction. He needed constant reassurance that it was not a true story. He then woke us up in the middle of the night, petrified.

"Sure," my spouse responded before I had even gotten my words out. "It's only a movie, how bad can it be?" The answer—Bad. Very bad. Ten minutes into the movie, I could not tell if I was watching a movie or CNN. The lines between fact and fiction are blurring. The movie came out in 2011, but the parallels between it and what we are experiencing now are uncanny. Dr. Sanjay Gupta even made an appearance in the movie, and he has been on the news every day for at least two weeks.

As I write this, it's hard to believe there was a time in my life when I thought writing was painful. I could not fathom why anyone would want to do it. Writing only 100 words was a punishment. (Why do teachers assign essays when kids get in trouble? It is like they want us to associate writing with suffering.) But now, keeping these posts short seems impossible. If someone told me back when I was in elementary school that I would want to be a writer, that I would find pleasure in putting words down on the page, I definitely would have hit them. And yet, here I am.

DAY 7

MARCH 22, 2020

This morning, we watched Governor Cuomo on the news and we were impressed with him. Compared to Trump, I suppose anyone with a brain and a bit of compassion would appear like a rock star. "He looks and acts presidential," I commented to my spouse. She nodded in agreement. He arrived at the press conference armed with facts and statistics. He spoke about where New York is in regard to fighting the virus and how bad it will get if he does not get the medical supplies he needs. He was calm in reassuring New Yorkers that panicking is not the solution. He was stern in reprimanding people in New York City for flooding to parks yesterday and not heeding the warnings and the call to practice social distancing. He also did not hold back in criticizing the president, predominantly his failure to do more to ensure that the states have what they need in order to save lives. My parents are in the vulnerable age group, and if I am going to have to worry about my parents at a time like this, I'm glad they live in a state with a responsible governor. A man who is fighting to save the residents of his state. A leader who wants to ensure that people do not die unnecessarily.

After breakfast, we braved a trip to ShopRite. For a Sunday afternoon, we could not believe how empty the parking lot was. The store was relatively calm as well. But some of the bread shelves were bare. There were no paper towels or toilet paper. (Although, later, I got a text from a friend saying she was able to buy them there. That they were in the back. I wonder if the store is intentionally hiding them to prevent a stampede.) And the ramen and rice aisle was completely empty. As we were checking out, one of the kids who works there told us that earlier a lady tried to buy several boxes of tissues. When he kindly told her that she could only buy one box, she flew into a rage and threw the box at him. It's not his fault that hoarders like her required the store to implement strict quotas on what you can buy.

DAY 8

MARCH 23, 2020

As you know, my parents were abroad on a cruise down in Patagonia until last week. Since they returned, I have been worried about them. My mom has been sick, but she and my dad keep telling me it is just a cold. In the midst of a pandemic, I cannot take anything for granted. I am full of anxiety. Last night, I messaged my dad asking how they were doing. His response unsettled me. Though I have been worried, I was taken aback when he responded that he was not doing well. He had lost his appetite and was unable to eat dinner because he was nauseous. My dad never loses his appetite. He is one of those people who gets extremely cranky if he does not eat regularly. I picked up the phone and called. "You need to get tested, to see if you have COVID," I told him.

"I'm not up for driving," his voice sounded heavy, drained.

"I'll drive into Queens and take you," I offered, since Mom does not drive.

"No, stay with your family," he insisted. "It's just a little nausea. It'll pass," he promised, but I was not so optimistic.

I did not sleep much. I kept waking up, fearing the worst. When my alarm finally went off this morning, I reached for my phone and messaged my dad. "How are you feeling?" I asked, then went out for my walk. When I returned, I checked to see if he had responded. He had not. After that, I checked my phone every ten minutes. He is always up early, so when a response didn't come in by seven, my anxiety mounted. Finally, he responded at seven fifty-three, "Ok, if you want to take me to get tested, I'll go." Of course I wanted to take him. I googled where to go. On the news, Governor Cuomo talks about the drive-up testing centers. I figured it could not be that hard to get my dad there. I found the number to call almost immediately. But New York is overly taxed with so many new cases every day, it was no surprise that I was put on hold. Earlier I had read that it is believed that New York has five percent of the cases world-wide. That is huge for just one state.

When a woman finally came on the line after about forty minutes, she gave me a brief interview. I answered the questions honestly, but she told me that my parents—if I was going to take my dad to get tested, I wanted to take my mom as well; they were on the same trip, they live together—were not a top priority. New York was overrun with people wanting to be tested so they had to be selective. I pleaded their case. They are old. They just got back from being overseas. But since they had not been in contact with anyone who definitely tested positive, they did not qualify to be tested. Furious but polite, I thanked the woman. It was only after I hung up that I remembered reading on Facebook that a priest from their neighborhood tested positive. They used to attend Mass every week, but it has been years since they were that diligent. Still, the information could be used to sway the test center. I called my dad and told him to call. He could talk more informatively about his symptoms. And I told him, when they asked if he was in contact with anyone, he should mention the church. He did. After sitting on hold for an eternity, he called me back. He managed to secure an appointment for himself and my mother. But the appointment could take up to three or four days to process. So, now we wait some more and hope that he does not get worse in the interim. In the meantime, my bag is packed. I am ready to go whenever they call.

It is a rainy, cold, and icky day. The poor weather makes it easier to be stuck in the house. But it is still a challenge. My son slept in. There seemed no reason to wake him up early, especially since I had been trying to sort things out for my parents. As always, he started his day reading with me. We are nearing the end of *Hound of the Baskervilles*. He is really enjoying the story thus far. But mostly it is the quirky main character, Sherlock Holmes, whom he likes.

For breakfast, I made French toast. While my son ate, we chatted with my parents on FaceTime. Dad did not look well, but he still tried to smile and sound cheerful for his only grandson.

Schoolwork followed breakfast. My son sulked about it, but so far, he has yet to have a melt-down. That does not mean he has been completely agreeable. He grumbled about the reading homework. He had to complete a passage online and then answer multiple-choice questions. I agree with him that reading passages that test comprehension are boring. But I will not admit it to him. You may find this hard to believe, but there was a time I used to hate reading. In fact, back in my freshman year of high school, I nearly failed English. Failing in my school was seventy-four, and one marking period, I came home with a seventy-five. Needless to say, my parents were livid. To me, working hard to comprehend a novel seemed a pointless endeavor. The worst were the test prep passages—dry stories that were so disconnected from anything relevant to my life—and the stupid multiple-choice questions that followed. Questions that simply took too much effort to answer. I still cannot take those tests. Or rather, I can take them. Just don't expect me to pass them.

Things started to change in my sophomore year when I had Mr. Madri as a teacher. He changed my entire outlook. I am not exactly sure how he did it. The fact that I felt like an outcast, like I didn't quite belong, may have contributed to my sudden interest in books. How else could I escape my surroundings without actually leaving? Where else would I find sanctuary, a place where I could have friends and feel a sense of purpose? Books became my friends when I got tired of being alone, tired of getting picked on, tired of being made fun of. Sometimes, I wonder how different my teen years would have been if there were queer books back then, if someone had handed me one. If I had seen myself in the pages of a novel, would I have learned to understand and accept myself sooner? My guess is that I would have. But alas, there were no lesbian books on the shelves of the Catholic school, so I read *Flowers in the Attic* instead.

In Madri's class, I did so well that when it came time to select courses for the following year, he refused to sign off on my English class until I selected honors. My parents were incredulous. They did not want me to take honors. They feared it would be too much. That it might overwhelm me. But eventually they relented. I then went on to major in English Literature at New York University.

But I still get it. I still understand why my son is rebelling against the assignment. I sent a message to his principal asking to do a modified homeschool curriculum without having to officially un-enroll him from school. My son might still complain, but reading a novel and responding to high-level questions would definitely be less painful—for both of us.

We were sitting down to dinner when Dad messaged me, "I have a fever, 104."

Immediately, I called him. "You need to take Tylenol," I advised.

"It doesn't work. It never works," he grumbled. "Besides, we don't have any."

I agree. Tylenol does absolutely nothing for pain. I do not care what the doctors say. But it does reduce a fever. However, with my dad's aversion to it, I was not surprised they didn't have it in the house. "Mom should call Debby," I suggested. "See if she has any." Debby was a neighbor and my mother's friend.

It turned out, she also didn't have Tylenol either. So I did the only thing I could do. Without finishing dinner—I was too panicked to eat more—I ran out to the pharmacy. Tylenol, apparently, disappeared along with all the toilet paper. All they had was a small travel-size container. I bought that, along with some generic pills.

From the pharmacy, I drove right into the epicenter of the pandemic in the United States. The drive to New York City never went so fast. There were hardly any cars on the road. Not a surprise since we are on a modified lockdown and Governor Murphy instituted a curfew. I sailed through Staten Island, which is often a parking lot at the tail end of rush hour. And when I got to Woodhaven Boulevard, it was eerily deserted. I felt like I was in one of those end-of-the-world movies where nearly everyone has died, and nothing remains but shadows and silence. The last time I did a spur-of-the-moment drive into New York was back in November when I decided I absolutely had to resume studying Taekwondo. I started years ago, when I lived in Korea and managed to earn a blue belt before leaving. My son's instructor told me he would let me pick up where I left off, but it would probably be good if I could locate my belt. Locate my belt? A belt I had not needed in two decades. Well, if I saved it, and it was a big *if*, it would be at my parents' house. And so, on a Sunday morning, I drove out to Queens. The minute I arrived, I tore into the boxes that held my keepsakes, boxes my mother meticulously stored in my closet. Shockingly, I unearthed some of my belts. Doing a little excited tap dance, I held the blue belt aloft. I still had it. That afternoon, my mother told my father that I was the happiest she had seen me in a long time.

This evening, I was much more somber. I got to my parents' house and did not hug anyone. I gave Dad the Tylenol and a thermometer. The one they have is a relic from back when I was a kid. They asked me to bring the one we have on hand for my son. I gave Mom instructions on how to use it, and it read Dad's temperature at 101.9 degrees. Not as bad as 104. Dad looked terrible. But he is still breathing fine. Tomorrow I am going to have to convince him to call his doctor.

On the way home, I spoke to my brother—who lives down in Nashville—to update him on Dad's condition. He said that he read online that the test centers in New York have stopped testing people. They are just telling people they will call with an appointment to appease them. New York is just too overwhelmed. I guess Cuomo is not entirely honest after all. On the radio, I heard that 12,000 people in New York City have tested positive. And 1,800 hospital beds are already occupied. The urgency in Mayor DeBlasio's and Cuomo's pleas to the Federal Government was suddenly personal. The deaths tallied on CNN were not just numbers, they were people with families in mourning, families missing them.

My brother is worried. I am worried. Everyone seems worried, except Dad.

DAY 9

MARCH 24, 2020

I did not sleep last night. I was too shaken. I think I half expected my phone to ring in the middle of the night. My son could not fall asleep either. When I got home, he was in bed, but he was wide awake. When I finished writing my daily entry, he was still awake. Then, at two thirty-five this morning, he woke me up. I think he was worried about his grandfather. "I need cuddles," he told me as he pushed me aside. I did, too, so he cuddled next to me. He fell asleep. I did not. At five o'clock, my alarm sounded. As always, I got up to work out. But I was too tired to stay awake when I finished. After my workout, I collapsed into bed and crashed. I got a solid hour of sleep until my spouse woke me up. Today, I have to teach. I have discussion boards to get up for my classes and papers to grade.

My son is in full-on rebellion again this morning. I am supposed to be teaching, interacting with my students, and commenting on their papers, but my son resents this time spent with "kids" other than him. Every time I turn to my computer in an attempt to read a paper, he erupts into a tirade. "You need to help me, and only me. Put your computer away and pay attention to me," he shouted when I told him he had to respond to his ELA questions in full sentences. Then, after I tried to help him with the final question, explaining exactly what he was supposed to do and how he was supposed to do it, he screamed, "Why don't you ever help me? Why don't you ever give me five minutes?" This, after I did exactly what he was accusing me of never doing. And then, when I tried to push through the tantrum to get at least one student paper read, he yelled, "I should be the most important person in your life. Me. You should pay attention to me. And Grandpa. You can help him, but I should be second." Our condo is too small for me to go anywhere to simply let him calm down. We are both stuck in his room while my spouse is on conference calls.

It's an early spring day. I wanted my son to get some exercise and fresh air, so we went out for another bike ride. I'm so glad my parents got him that bike for his birthday. It's allowed us to have a little freedom, a little peace in an otherwise stressful time. I enjoy biking. I always have, but my son has never had my stamina. I could have gone for a long while, but after twenty minutes, he was done. He was tired and thirsty. It was still early, still lovely outside, so I insisted on a game of box ball. Three minutes into the game, my son started complaining. I wasn't hitting the ball hard enough. I was hitting too hard. I wasn't hitting it high enough. In fact, I wasn't playing right at all. Wait a minute. Wasn't I the one who taught him how to play? I pointed that out, and in a huff, he ran inside and turned on the television before I could stop him. "You still have to do your math work," I reminded him. A gentle reminder that ignited his fuse.

"I hate you. I hate being home. I hate everything. I haven't been able to do anything fun all day."

I thought biking was fun, but I wisely refrained from saying so. Instead, I tried, "None of us have done anything fun. I've been trying to work. Trying to get you to do work. And getting nothing done. This whole thing isn't fun for anyone."

He glared at me. "Yeah, well, you're not a kid. This isn't your childhood being totally ruined." Okay, he had me there. My childhood wasn't marred by a world-wide pandemic made worse by a beloved grandfather who was sick and an incompetent buffoon of a president.

Speaking of buffoons, do you remember a week or so ago when Vice President Pence promised that anyone who wanted a coronavirus test would be able to get one? Well, he lied. No surprise there. The current administration has lied to us repeatedly from day one. What's troubling about this lie is that it's personal. I want my parents to get tested. They want to get tested. I want to know if my dad has the virus or just the flu because it would alter my level of anxiety. But the promise he got on the phone yesterday, that someone would call back with a testing date and time, seems to have been a lie. An attempt, as my brother said, to pacify my father. That is unacceptable to me. What kind of person—no, what kind of Christian—stands in front of a nation and lies, a lie big enough to get people killed? I've despised Trump from the beginning, but in the last couple of days my rage has risen to new heights. He and Pence are causing more chaos by refusing to listen to science and reason. By refusing to be honest. Who knew I could detest someone this much?

My spouse came home from a pharmacy run and sat with our son to work on his math homework. She had about as much luck as I had earlier doing his ELA homework. He rebels furiously against the Kahn Academy videos and the quizzes that follow. "This is a waste of my time" has become his mantra for math. I, too, hate learning through videos. I don't have the attention span. I struggle when things are not hands-on. It's the conversation I need. Or rather the ability to ask questions and have them answered directly. In this new way of learning, my son fails every quiz he takes, not because he doesn't understand the material, but because he can't be bothered to take the time to do it right.

I called Dad before dinner. He still has a fever, but he says he is feeling better than he did yesterday. Mom said he's not as lethargic. I'm hoping this is a good sign, but I don't think I'll actually be able to relax until his fever breaks and he doesn't need the Tylenol anymore.

DAY 10

MARCH 25, 2020

We don't do technology well in this family at all. I have no idea if it's nature or nurture. Are our brains simply not wired to adapt as well as some other peoples' brains, or do we just learn to avoid new things because we are comfortable with the old? This morning, we FaceTimed Mom and Dad as we always do in the morning. We started when my son was little so that he could chat with his grandparents and so that they could see him. It always reminds me of *The Jetsons*. I'm sure you watched the cartoon in your youth. I remember being a kid and watching the show and being awed by the prospect of actually being able to see the person you are talking to while on the phone. I wanted it so badly. To be able to call up my grandparents (who lived down the block and around the corner, so it's not like I was starved to see them) and look at them. What a miraculous invention that would be. And now, my son lives it. He indulges in video calls all the time. So okay, maybe we aren't completely averse to all technology, but I digress.

"How are you feeling?" I asked Dad, noticing that he looked better, although he was still coughing.

"Fine. I still have a fever, but my temperature dropped. However, your mother or I did something to the thermometer."

"What did you do? Do you need me to get you another one?"

"No," he shook his head, pausing as he coughed, his body leaning forward, his face reddening. "It still works. But only in Celsius."

"What?" On Monday, I had given him our thermometer. It's digital. You press a button to turn it on, put it under your tongue, and when it beeps, it displays your temperature. But it's definitely more steps than those old school mercury ones that have no batteries or buttons. "I didn't even know it could switch between Fahrenheit and Celsius," I said. "But you can probably switch it back."

Dad shrugged, "Probably, but I don't know how." So, now he has the additional step of having to convert Celsius to Fahrenheit in order to get an accurate reading—one that makes sense.

As Dad was telling me this, two stories collided in my memory. The first—and this is why my son and spouse were chuckling in the background—was a few years ago when we drove to Lancaster, Pennsylvania, to visit James Buchanan's house. Our son is passionately interested in the history of presidents and wants to visit each of their houses. Buchanan was one of our early visits. My spouse, as always, was driving. I was in charge of navigating via her cell phone. At some point, I hit the wrong thing. And suddenly, instead of being three minutes away, we were twenty. "How can that be?" I exclaimed. She tore the phone from my hand, agitation oozing out of her. But she quickly diagnosed the problem. I had inadvertently switched it from driving to walking directions. At the time, she was steaming mad. Now, we laugh about it.

Second, I remembered an Earnest Hemingway short story I read years ago in his collection, *The Snows of Kilimanjaro and Other Stories*. "A Day's Wait" is about a young boy who gets sick in Europe. When the doctor arrives and examines him, he declares that the boy has a temperature of 102. The young boy bravely takes this information, curls up into himself, and then proceeds to spend the day waiting to die. The doctor had read his temperature in Fahrenheit, but the boy, used to Celsius, thought his fever was terminal.

This morning, while the corn bread was in the oven, I told my son to work on his math. He immediately launched into a tantrum about having to watch more Kahn Academy videos and do more "stupid" problems. In less than five minutes, my son and spouse were yelling at each other. Eventually, my son settled down and did the work, though I am willing to bet it was rushed and ultimately did not reflect his ability. After breakfast, we moved on to writing a persuasive letter for ELA. His bitterness and resentment carried over. I tried to explain how he could expand his thoughts in each body paragraph, but he launched into an attack. "I don't need another lecture."

"I'm not lecturing," I pointed out. "I'm trying to explain."

But to him, they are the same. "It's not like I'm ever going to write a persuasive letter in real life," he shot back.

"Actually, you are. You will write many of them. Persuasion is the backbone of research essays, which you will write in college," I argued.

"Then I won't go to college."

Yep, I'd say that went well. But once he calmed down, he did listen and incorporate my advice. Perhaps we can have a bit of calm for the rest of the day.

My son doesn't dress like the average ten-year-old. He wears button-down shirts, ties, and sports jackets to school—public school.

When school shut down, we had to go online and order him sweatpants. Hanging out at home day after day, he needed comfortable lounge clothes, and he didn't have any. This afternoon, he has a Zoom conference with his teacher and some of the kids in his class. The moment I reminded him about the meeting, he ran into his room and started to get dressed—button-down shirt and jeans. "What?" I exclaimed. "You're going to make me iron during the pandemic?" My spouse laughed.

My son responded, "Yeah, I have to look nice if I'm going to see my class." Oy vey! A slice of normalcy in an otherwise mixed-up world. How can I complain? I'm happy he's smiling. It was the first time all week he was dressed before noon, and the meeting wasn't until two-thirty.

He wasn't smiling when I tried to connect him to the Zoom meeting. As I've stated, numerous times, I suck at figuring out technology. The easiest part was downloading the app. That part I got simple enough. I even connected to the meeting. However, there was no video. It took me a while to figure out how to use the video function. In the process, I accidentally put it on mute. When my son's teacher commented that he was on mute, he threw down the phone. On the verge of tears, he declared he was too embarrassed to stay on the call. Picking up the phone, I fiddled around a bit until I eventually tapped on the right place, but I have no clue what that place was. He sat on the stairs, his "office," but he sounded melancholy answering his teacher's questions. He looked bored while he listened to his classmates. But at least, for a few minutes, he wasn't sitting around the house complaining there was nothing to do or shouting at us for making him do work. When he got off the phone, he told me, "That's not what I expected. I thought it was going to be like the calls Mommy does with her classes. I thought we'd go over homework." He was disappointed because it turned out to be more of a social meeting than an educational one.

It was a cold and damp day, but I wanted to get him out of the house for a bit. Fresh air and exercise, a slice of sanity, perhaps normalcy. My spouse needed her prescription filled, so I suggested a walk to the pharmacy—about a mile from where we live. My son does not like to walk, but he loves peanut butter cups. So I bribed him. I told him if he walked, I'd buy him candy. He acquiesced. We had an extremely pleasant walk—dare I say fun. For the short time we were out, he was playful and funny. He was dancing and joking, pushing me into bushes and laughing. Yes, laughing. There was a sparkle in his eyes and a smile on his lips. At the pharmacy, I picked up my spouse's prescription and looked for Tylenol, figuring it might not be bad to have on hand in case one of us got sick and needed it. But the shelves were bare. We each got a chocolate peanut butter egg and sat outside to eat them. My son unwrapped his and held it out to me so I could tap the tip of mine to his. "Cheers," he said, biting into it.

Dad continued to feel better. I spoke to him before dinner. He had just finished eating a bowl of strawberries and whipped cream. His nausea had subsided, and his fever broke. He thinks he has the virus, but he feels he is on the mend. I'll feel better when he stops coughing. Mom, who for days told me she was just battling a cold, now tells me she thinks she, too, might have had the virus. Along with her cold, she was dizzy and nauseous. At one point, her cough was worse than my dad's, but she didn't want me to worry. Neither of them did.

After his bath, my son decided it was time to switch from winter pajamas to spring pajamas. The first day of spring has come and gone, and I didn't even take note. I think it's the first time I completely forgot to pay attention to the arrival of my favorite season.

As I was heading to bed, a text came in from Dad, "Temperature back up, but not too high."

Snapshot Rewind (Writing just about the present can be a bit depressing. Sitting at home, I am telling stories of my childhood to my son. So I'm going to add them here at the end of my daily posts. A tidbit of who I was before I became me. A break from the news, the complaints, the temper tantrums.)

September 1974: I was born on a busy day in the labor and delivery room. Lots of babies drew their first breaths the same day as me, many of them girls. As a result, there were no clean pink receiving blankets when it was my turn to need one. The nurse, therefore, broke protocol and wrapped me in a blue blanket. When she presented me to my father, he was livid. He snapped at the nurse, stating that a baby girl should not be wrapped like a boy. The nurse apologized, explaining her dilemma. Dad asked if there were any yellow blankets, and nurse quickly exchanged the blue blanket for a yellow. Dad didn't want anyone to think I was a son. Oh, the irony. Perhaps it's the nurse's fault. If I hadn't initially been swaddled in blue, perhaps I'd have grown up to prefer girl clothes, girl colors.

DAY 11

MARCH 26, 2020

I am pissed off my parents aren't getting tested. That whomever my dad spoke to on the phone lied to him. On the news, I watch the numbers go up hourly, especially the numbers in New York. So, who is getting tested? I read about celebrities with minor symptoms getting tested, and athletes—who are in prime physical condition and obviously not old—getting tested without any symptoms at all. How rich do you need to be to get tested? How famous? Why should an actor or a basketball star get preferential treatment? Why are they more important than my parents?

At seven o'clock, I woke my son up as I always do, and he read to me for a half hour. He has one page—ONE—left in *Hound of the Baskervilles*, but he refused to finish it. He pointed out the fact that he had already read for a half hour—his allotted reading time—and, therefore, didn't have to read more. Grrrr. Sometimes he can be so infuriating. But he was tired, so he got off the couch and went back to bed. Within seconds, he was sound asleep. When he finally got up around nine forty-five, I got his breakfast ready and then called my parents to see if they wanted to FaceTime. Dad wasn't up to it. He said he didn't feel well. His speech was slurred. I begged him to call his doctor, but he refused. He called on Monday, and the doctor wanted nothing to do with him. A doctor my dad has seen for decades. A doctor my dad has always raved about. A doctor who has always been attentive in the past.

A tsunami of panic raced through me. He wouldn't call the doctor. But he didn't sound right. He was feeling worse than ever, and he didn't want to talk to his grandson, that alone was a red flag. I didn't know what to do. So,I called my brother. He advised me to call my dad's doctor. I did, and the result was disheartening. The woman who answered the phone said the doctor had been out of the office for two weeks. He is "feeling under the weather" and not responding to any of his patients. Great! So what do I do? She advised me to take him to an urgent care facility. My brother texted me the address of one near my parents, the one closest to their house, but then I spoke to a friend of mine who is a nurse. Her advice was to call ahead first. Many urgent care facilities are not accepting patients who they suspect might have the coronavirus. Now what? How crappy is this? To be in the midst of a medical emergency and not be able to get medical care. She said the best course of action was to take him to the ER, but only if his lips were blue or if he had trouble breathing. There is no treatment. She told me as long as he can breathe, they'd send him home anyway. The best we could do was keep him hydrated and monitor his temperature.

How did it get to this point? A person is sick. He wants a definitive diagnosis and the advice of a doctor, but the medical profession is so overrun with more urgent cases that unless he needs a ventilator, no one will even talk to him. And just like that, it doesn't matter how good your insurance is. The coronavirus has equalized the playing field. Except for the ultra-rich and famous. I'm sure their families aren't sitting at home worried the way I am. I'm sure they are getting top care even if their symptoms are milder than my dad's.

I am a terrible mother. My son asked for more cornbread for breakfast because he was still hungry. I evidently toasted it for him and buttered it, but one of the many calls I was making and fielding regarding my dad, distracted me before I could carry the dish from the kitchen counter to the dining room table. Two hours after he initially sat down to eat, I walked into the kitchen and found the cornbread, now cold, sitting next to the toaster oven. If I can't remember to feed my own kid, how can I possibly be productive tending to my classes? I have already fallen behind, but I do not have the mental capacity right now to focus on discussion boards and research papers. Suddenly, nothing matters, except for Dad making it through this.

Sitting down at my desk, I cried. All week I've managed to hold it in, but not today. At least my son behaved. I don't know if it's because I was too preoccupied to make him do schoolwork and so he got to watch too much television. Or, maybe, silence is his way of processing the fear we are both experiencing. If Dad doesn't make it, it will devastate me, but it will devastate my son more.

My spouse was excited this morning (before I found out about my dad) because "I get to go to work today." I'm not sure I've ever heard those words spoken with a ring of enthusiasm. But work was a reason to get out of the house. A reason to break up the monotony of her day teaching online. A reason to get dressed, in real clothes, not lounging attire. She wasn't going to there to teach, obviously. Schools are closed. But the administration opened the building today so teachers could come in and pick up anything they needed, anything they may have forgotten in their rushed exit two weeks ago. If teachers wanted to go in, they needed to put in a request. The administrators arranged for three teachers to enter the building at a time, and they were only allowed fifteen minutes to collect their things. When she reached her classroom door, there was crime scene type tape across it labeled with the date her room was cleaned, disinfected to kill any coronavirus germs.

When she got home, my son and I grabbed our rollerblades and drove to the local bike path. As we rollerbladed, my son asked, "Are we going to see Grandpa this weekend?"

"No, he's still sick. We can't see him until he is better and not contagious. If he has the virus, I don't want you getting sick."

"But what if something happens and I never see him again?"

"You will."

"But what if I don't?"

"You will."

"Okay, but if something happens to him and I never see him again, I will never forgive you."

I sucked in my breath and tried not to cry. But I know how he feels. I was ten when my grandmother died. And I can't remember the last time I hugged her. She hugged me often. I remember her hugging me, but I don't remember the last time, and that makes me feel like I lost something special.

Before dinner, we FaceTimed Mom and Dad. Dad sounds better than he did this morning. His temperature is back down. He is still feeling rotten, but his lips are most definitely not blue. I am still wound entirely too tight. But I've always been an overly emotional person. The stress of this new life is not going to alleviate that. However, I found a few moments of calm and quiet after we ate. My son and I curled up together and I read him his new *Ranger Rick* magazine. Cuddles and reading make everything better—at least for a little while.

Snapshot Rewind

1982 (second grade): I walked through the front door with my mother and younger brother after school. The minute I dropped my schoolbag from my shoulder, I shouted, "I'm not doing my homework. It's stupid and I hate it."

"What is it that you have to do?" my mother asked, her jaw set tight as she tried to channel every last bit of her patience.

"I have to write a paragraph." I stomped into the dining room where I did my homework every afternoon.

"On what?" my mother asked.

"My favorite meal."

"Oh, that's easy."

"No, it's not," I argued. "I have to write a whole paragraph. Five sentences. It's too much."

"Well, let's start with the first sentence." My mother calmly took out my notebook and a pencil. She set them down on the table. "What's your favorite meal?"

"Daddy's cream turkey."

"Well, there you go. That's your first sentence."

Squeezing my pencil and pressing down hard, I began to write.

With patience I've never been able to replicate, my mother walked me through the assignment, minimizing the pain of having to put my thoughts on paper.

I think of that moment often—especially these last two weeks—when my son is throwing a tantrum about schoolwork. I don't know how much I believe in karma, but watching my son pitch a fit about writing makes me wonder if it's a thing. If I somehow cursed myself with a mini-me. It also makes me wonder, what does he despise now that he might learn to love later?

DAY 12

MARCH 27, 2020

It's never good when a phone call wakes you in the middle of the night. At four thirty-three, my phone rang. I bolted up in bed and answered it, knowing immediately it was my mom. My dad was worse. He had the chills. He was shaking uncontrollably.

"But can he breathe?" I asked, frantic.

"Yes," my mother assured me. "But he needs to go to the hospital. We called an ambulance. They won't take him to Columbia Presbyterian. They'll only take him to the closest one."

"I'm on my way. I gotta shower, then I'll get in the car."

"Don't panic," my mother said as I hung up the phone, but it was too late. I was already panicking.

An ambulance would have taken my dad to Elmhurst. I didn't want him there. Neither did my mother. It's a public hospital. Yesterday, thirteen people died at that hospital. They are already overrun with coronavirus patients. My parents have always gone to Columbia Presbyterian—it's where their doctor is. They have Dad's records. We knew he had that working to his advantage. They are also one of the top hospitals in the nation.

I was on the road by five. There was no traffic. There are lots of sucky things about this pandemic, but the lack of traffic is certainly something I could get used to. Traveling over the bridges, without concern of how bad the back-up will be, is blissful—or would be, if circumstances were different.

But the minute I arrived at my parents' house, it was evident that my dad was *not* breathing well. He struggled to get down the stairs, moving down on his butt instead of his feet. He was visibly shaking. His speech was even more slurred than yesterday. He was barely coherent. My mother did not want me to get near him because of the virus. He was about to get into my car, where exposure was unavoidable, but they were still trying to protect me. My mom put gloves on his hands and a mask on his face—construction masks that she bought years ago in an attempt to quell her allergies when gardening.

Mom helped Dad into my car, both of them sitting in the back, trying to keep as much distance from me as possible. I drove over the Queensboro Bridge—in the heart of what was once rush hour—and there was no traffic. I flew into Manhattan. At the hospital, I couldn't leave my car at the entrance, so I dropped Mom and Dad off. I didn't kiss Dad goodbye. I didn't hug him. I was being cautious. I didn't want to increase my chances of bringing the virus home to my son. But, as I watched Dad awkwardly shuffle into the hospital, I felt the rumbling of regret. I should have chased after him and pulled him into my arms, but I didn't. I let fear get the better of me. And when the hospital door shut behind him, I knew I had made a mistake, one that would haunt me forever.

I drove around and eventually parked illegally to wait for Mom to call. When she did, I picked her up. She looked calm and composed, though disappointed they would not let her stay with Dad.

"How is he?" I asked.

"Good." I saw her nod, as if in a trance, in the rear-view mirror. "They put him on oxygen. He wasn't breathing well. So they put him on oxygen. But he's okay."

"Are you sure?"

"Yes." But as I drove, the nightmare of the previous night unfolded. Mom told me that he had collapsed twice—once in the living room, once in the bathroom. She had trouble picking him up, but she managed. His stomach was wrecked. He couldn't sleep. He couldn't get comfortable. His breathing didn't sound right.

His breathing didn't sound right. "What? Why didn't you call me?"

"Your father is so thick. So stubborn. He kept telling me he was okay."

I should have taken him to the hospital yesterday. I knew I should have gone yesterday.

"He's going to be okay," Mom promised me. (The same promise I made my son yesterday, but now I wasn't feeling quite so optimistic.)

Before taking Mom home, I took her grocery shopping. While we were in the meat section, my dad called. I was happy to hear him, though he sounded terrible, like he was struggling to process words.

"I tried calling your mother, but she didn't answer," he wheezed, his voice heavy, words unevenly spaced.

"Would you like to talk to her?"

"No, just let her know they're putting me on a ventilator," he said as I stood frozen by the poultry, struggling to breathe. It was as if all the oxygen had been sucked out of the store.

In shock, I nodded, even though he couldn't see me. "Okay, I'll talk to you later," I stupidly said, as if it were any ordinary conversation. And then I hung up, without saying "I love you." Another regret that would torment me.

At my parents' house, we waited for the doctor to call. I had too much nervous energy. Plus, I was trying to avoid being inside, surrounded by deadly germs. So, I went for a walk. While I was out, I called my mom to see if she had heard anything. She did, but she was reluctant to tell me until I got home. Good news doesn't need to wait, so I insisted she tell me immediately.

"It's not good." She sounded distant and far away. "His kidneys are failing. He needs dialysis."

"What does that mean? Will he make it?"

"The doctor's not sure. Sometimes people pull through after dialysis. But with the virus? It all happened so fast."

Too fast. We had plans. We were supposed to wait out this pandemic together in Long Island. We were supposed to go to Disney. I promised my son he'd see Dad again.

"We should have taken him yesterday," I said, berating myself.

"The doctor said it wouldn't have mattered. In all likelihood, they would have sent him home if he wasn't this bad."

"Sent him home. But—"

"It's the virus," Mom cut me off. "Things are different. Even the doctors are trying to figure it all out."

"I'll be home soon." I hung up and cried like I hadn't cried in years. Not since my grandmother died. Not since I was my son's age and I lost the grandparent I loved most. The grandparent who meant the world to me, as my father means the world to my son. Dad is his rock. His idol. His hero. And now ...

I couldn't stop the tears.

Forget what you see on the news. This is the face of the coronavirus. A ten-year-old curled up on the couch crying. A beloved grandson, dressed up like a gangster and shooting imaginary enemies because he can't kill the real one. A ten-year-old whose heart is breaking. A little boy who was looking forward to another summer on the beach with his grandfather. The pandemic isn't about statistics or a failed federal government. It certainly isn't a hoax. It's about one of the people I love most being taken from me way too soon.

Early in the year, I had suggested Dad not plan a Disney trip this coming summer. My son's behavior didn't warrant it. Dad argued, "Your mother and I aren't getting any younger. I want to take him before I'm not here." But he was healthy. A week ago, he was healthy and happy and looking forward to Easter with his grandson, the greatest joy in his life. Now, none of us may ever see him again. He very well may not get that one last trip to Florida, one final chance to spoil his grandson.

And because my mother may be infected with the virus, and the house most certainly is, I can't be with my mother and my son. I cannot physically be a support system for both of them. But my mother cannot be alone. Not now. Not at a time like this. So I will stay with her. My son will have his other mother—for now. Until I can be with him again.

But I did go home briefly to pick up clothes. I ran out so quickly this morning I even forgot my coat. I returned to Queens at five-thirty p.m.. In normal times, I'd have sat in traffic for hours trying to get over the bridges. But again, no one was on the road, no one but me, but I'd gladly sit in hours upon hours of traffic if it meant I could see my father again.

As I write, I am home with Mom. She is sitting in the living room, flipping through channels on the television, but every show upsets her. Neither of us can tolerate the news. Our world is crumbling. The outside world feels irrelevant. Happy shows upset her because she is so far from being happy. Depressing shows make her feel worse. And schmaltzy shows remind her of my dad. He loved schmaltzy shows; the more schmaltzy, the better. They always have a happy ending, and we may not.

Mom is reminiscing. Talking about Dad. I can't count how many times she has told me that my father was super proud and ecstatic that I named my son after him. He told everyone, she said, with a big smile that he has one grandson, but that one grandson has his name. "You couldn't have given him a better gift," she said. My son was the best thing that ever happened to my dad. He wanted to be the best grandfather a kid could have. It saddened him that he never knew his own grandparents.

The doctor called—again. My dad is not getting any better. He's bad. He's on a ventilator. He's medicated and sleeping. He is not in pain. But his kidneys aren't working. If he survives the night, they will start him on dialysis.

All I have eaten today is ice cream. Once upon a time, I believed that ice cream could solve any problem. That it could ease your sorrow. Make you feel better. I was wrong.

I'm now drinking a Black Russian. However, that's just making me think of Dad. The bottle of Kahlua in the liquor cabinet was unopened. Dad bought it just for me. Black Russians are my drink. But I was supposed to be drinking this cocktail with him, not alone. We always had cocktails together. But now …

This is my regret: I wish I had gotten out of the car and hugged Dad before my mother walked him into the emergency room. I'd give anything to hug him again. I wish I could talk to him. I wish I could tell him—at least one more time—that I love him.

Snapshot Rewind
2010: As a child, I was always closer to my dad than my brother was. Or perhaps that's just my perception. Anyway, I once told my dad that I was upset he named my brother, and not me, Gary. I am older. I should have been the junior. My father explained that someday I would grow up and get married. I'd change my name. It was a fact; names did not get passed through the maternal line. But I didn't marry a man. I never changed my name, and so I proved him wrong. When my son was born, I named my son after him. And even though a child named after his grandfather should be II, I made my son III. It made sense—to me. My brother is a Jr. My son is the third generation. Technically, my dad is probably

right. Traditionally speaking, my son can't be a III. But I'm a lesbian. I can simultaneous defy and follow tradition. I can make up my own rules.

DAY 13

MARCH 28, 2020

Daddy always made everything right. Whenever something was wrong in my life, he fixed it. I could always count on him to be there. When I was at my worst, he picked me up, hugged me, and set me back on my feet. But now, I can't do the same for him. I can't make him well. I can't force his kidneys to work or make his lungs cooperate. I can't kill the virus that is killing him. I should have been more persistent on Thursday. I should have driven to Queens and forced him into my car. I should not have listened to him when he told me he could breathe. That he was getting better. That he was fine.

Last night, I didn't sleep in my room, the room I grew up in. The room that holds all my childhood memories—Dad painting the walls (pink when I was a kid, green when I got older). Dad smiling at me when I added another athletic trophy to my collection. Dad fixing my Olivia Newton-John cassette when the tape spilled out of the plastic. Instead, I slept in what was once my brother's room, and has since become my son's room when we visit—and we visit often, so often that when my son was a toddler Dad bought him a new mattress. Hung on the wall beside the bed are a collection of collages, one for each year of my son's life. It's been my Christmas present to my parents ever since my son's first Christmas—a collage to highlight the places they took my son, the things they did with him, the memories they formed. There is one collage for each year, plus two from our trips to Disney. There's Dad holding my son next to the alpaca at the Bronx Zoo. Dad on the beach holding his one-year-old grandson's hand as they walk down to the water. Dad trick-or-treating with him the year hurricane Sandy displaced us. Dad and my son on the Dumbo ride at Disney. The three Garys sitting on the couch. (Dad loves having all three Garys together). Dad with his grandson at a Mets game, on a replica of the *Amistad*, and at the circus. And my son hugging his grandfather—there are many of those. I spent hours staring at the pictures and crying. Trying to reach my dad with unspoken words—thoughts, as if they could travel that far—to let him know that I'm thinking of him. Since I can't be with Dad, I guess I wanted to be near him in the only way I can be.

That's the worst part of this, that he's alone right now. I want to be with him, holding his hand, babbling on about everything and nothing just so that he could hear my voice and know that I am with him. But instead, Mom and I are here at home, feeling absolutely helpless. My mom got a call from the hospital asking if my father practices a religion. When she said Catholic, they assured her a priest would pray for him. But because of the virus (which the doctor confirmed he has) and the need to contain it, the priest can't go into the room; he can only stand outside the glass. And if my dad gets worse, the priest can't even go in to administer Last Rites. A Catholic his entire life, my dad would be denied this last comfort because of a freaking disease that is wreaking havoc across the globe.

"Was he wearing his crucifix yesterday?" I asked my mom when she hung up the phone.

She shook her head, "He left it at home. With his wedding ring." Dad got the crucifix years ago. I remember going with him and my mother to a jewelry store to pick it out. He was so excited. I had no idea men could get that excited about jewelry, but Dad was very attached to it. He always wore it, except to the beach because he didn't want it to accidentally fall off in the water.

What compounds my misery at the moment is the fact that to-day—March 28—has been marked on our calendar since early December. My son was supposed to be competing in a tournament up in Hollis, New Hampshire. But not only were we excited about the competition, the escape out of New Jersey for a weekend, we were also looking forward to a family reunion. Back in December, my son competed at a different tournament in Nashua, NH. My dad toyed with the idea of driving up to watch, but it's a long drive, so he decided against it. He promised he'd wait for a tournament closer to home and then come. The day before we left, I posted on Facebook that I was looking forward to getting out of New Jersey. A friend commented, asking where we were going. When I responded, Nashua, my second cousin, Tani, replied that she lived only twenty minutes away.

Okay, I need to back up a bit here. Last Thanksgiving, when I was visiting my parents, I asked my dad who a particular woman on Facebook was. I had noticed her reacting to quite a few posts and pictures that I had tagged him in. He explained that Tani is my second cousin, the daughter of his first cousin, Anna, who he hadn't seen since he was twelve. I knew I had distant relatives; names had been bounced around and posted on Kerry's—another cousin—ancestry tree. But until that moment, it was all somewhat abstract. So I sent my cousin, and her mother, friend requests. This was the cousin who later stated that she lived only twenty minutes away from Nashua. A month before, I didn't even know she existed. I couldn't miss this opportunity to possibly meet her. So I invited her to the tournament, and after an exchange of messages, she said that she and her mom would come. I was excited—and nervous—to meet family. It ended up being an extremely pleasant

61

afternoon. They watched my son compete in a black belt ring for the first time, and then Anna took us all out for dinner. It was wonderful getting to know them. The conversation could have stretched out even longer, but we had a long drive home. When I told my dad that we got together with his family, he regretted not driving up to the tournament. So, we made plans to make it happen next time. Today. Dad was going to drive up to watch the tournament and then we were all going to get together—a mini-reunion, which now, may never take place. To think I had been looking forward to today for months, having no idea what this day would actually bring.

This morning, I went for a walk. But I felt like Pigpen from *Peanuts*, except I wasn't surrounded by a cloud of dirt, I was surrounded by a cloud of germs. I stayed away from everyone, walking around the cemetery, figuring that was the safest place to be. And as I walked, I remembered when Dad taught me to drive. The first time he let me get behind the wheel of his car, he took me to the cemetery. When he got out of the car to let me slip into the driver's seat, he announced, "You can practice here. They're all dead, so you don't have to worry about killing anyone." That memory made me smile, and then the tears came—again.

It sucks sitting at home and waiting. Every time the phone rings, my heart leaps, my knees buckle. I fear each ring will bring bad news. But waiting is all I can do—and writing. When I started this blog, it was supposed to be a fun endeavor. A way for my son and I to bond during the pandemic. An avenue by which we could vent our frustrations. A time capsule of our thoughts and feelings. I had no idea it would become a form of therapy, a way to keep friends and family updated about the greatest tragedy of my life. It was supposed to be a lighthearted activity. It wasn't supposed to be a record of my heart breaking.

I spoke to my son via video chat. He isn't feeling well. His stomach hurts, and he feels like he might throw up. He is slumped on the couch. It pains me that I can't be with him. That I can't hold him and cuddle with him. It sucks that I can't be with both my mother and my son. But at least he has my spouse. And his stomach probably hurts from all the crap he ate yesterday. He's crushed, so my spouse spoiled him with food in an attempt to keep his spirits from sinking too low.

The doctor called. Dad has bacteria in his blood—a secondary infection—which is exacerbating the symptoms of the virus. They are running some tests to discern more while giving him antibiotics. They are also treating him with hydroxychloroquine. I am sure you've heard of it in the news. It's the malaria medicine that is being used experimentally to treat COVID-19 patients. Trump had touted it as a lifesaving medication. I can't believe we have reached a point where I am hoping he was right about something. I really like my dad's doctor. Despite the horrors she is dealing with and how busy she must be, each time she calls, she takes her time answering our questions. Not once has she tried to rush us off the phone. She is the most personable doctor I have ever dealt with. At a time like this, it is very much appreciated. As we were getting off the phone, she said that unless Dad took a turn for the worst, we wouldn't hear from her until tomorrow. So now, I pray the phone does not ring for the rest of the day.

As for Mom, she is terrified and sad. Last night, she refused to sleep in bed. The thought of being there without my dad next to her was depressing. Instead, she slept—or rather prayed through the night—in Dad's recliner in the living room. Perhaps it's her way of being closer to him.

Snapshot Rewind

2009: When I was little, my favorite bedtime story was *The Fourteen Bears of Summer and Winter*. I had Dad read it to me night after night. He would read all the bears' names with an exaggerated frustration that made me giggle. When I told him I was pregnant, before we knew if I was having a boy or a girl, he ordered a copy of the book. It was the first gift he gave his grandson.

DAY 14

MARCH 29, 2020

Last night, I was afraid to fall asleep, afraid that I might be woken up by a phone call I did not want to answer.

Now that I am up, all I can do is wait, and pray, and hope. I pace the floor, counting my footsteps, but even that doesn't calm me. My nerves are on over-drive, my hands shaking, my body vibrating. I've never wanted anything as badly as I want Dad to come home. I just can't fathom a world without him.

I'm waiting on two fronts. First, and most importantly, to hear from the doctor, to get an update. Secondly, I'm waiting to get sick. After picking up my dad and now living with my mom, I've been completely exposed to the virus. The incubation period is two weeks. I have twelve more days until I know how badly I have been affected. But that fear is easy enough to put out of my mind—at least for now. It's Dad I can't stop thinking about. I can't even read. I've tried. I read the same sentence over and over and it simply didn't compute. I'm supposed to be teaching, but how can I respond to emails when the words blur and fear grips me so tightly that I can't breathe? Writing is the only thing that calms me—slightly. It's the only time I can force my brain to focus; perhaps it's because I'm hyper-focusing on Dad. Through writing, I am channeling my energy to him.

Before Dad got sick, I had been watching the news obsessively. Now, I can't bear to turn it on. The president angers me. And the horror of the sick and dying is too much for me. I can't absorb any more sorrow.

Besides, I do not need to turn on the news to know how bad it is in New York City. A solemn silence fills the streets. There are no cars, no kids playing. I haven't even heard the Long Island Railroad, and it runs right behind my parents' house. But the silence is punctured repeatedly by the sound of sirens. They are nearly continuous. Men and women in ambulances being rushed to the hospital. I lay in bed at night, and I hear them. I walk, and ambulances race past me on the street. I sit in the living room, and they remind me that I am not alone in my sorrow. My pain.

I wait.

And wait.

And wait.

All this nervous energy and fear is like acid in my stomach. Unless there was bad news sooner, the doctor said she'd call between eleven-thirty and one. It is now two thirty-eight, and still no word. Every possible worst-case scenario is racing through my head. The horror is palpable. I may pace a hole in my parents' hardwood living room floor. I text my brother to let him know we still have no word. A few minutes later, he responds, "There is a lot going on at the hospital. No wonder they are delayed. They opened a second ICU in the OR that the surgeons are staffing while they're not doing elective procedures." I do not know how he knows. Perhaps research is his way of dealing with fear. Maybe the news does not repel him as it does me. Whatever the reason, that information eases my mother's worry. Not mine.

At two fifty-eight, the doctor calls. There is slight improvement with my dad, but the doctor cautioned us against getting too excited, too optimistic. Dad's kidneys are functioning, and his blood appears better, but he is still on the ventilator. It may be a while before they can consider taking him off of it. Hearing the news, it's like a valve opened, and the acid spilled out. I am suddenly hungry after not eating all day

Snapshot Rewind
1987: In the spring, I had my Confirmation. For Catholics, it's a big deal, a time to reaffirm your membership in the church. Because it is an important rite of passage, my mother wanted to buy me a suitable present. She recommended an expensive piece of jewelry—earrings, perhaps a necklace. But I've never been girly enough to want jewelry. Instead, because my entire life revolved around basketball, I wanted a basketball hoop in the backyard. My mother frowned. That's not what she had envisioned for her daughter. It's not what she wanted. But my father intervened. He knew his money would be better spent on something athletic. The weekend of my Confirmation, he dug a hole in the yard and set up the hoop. It was one of the best gifts I ever got, and I used it for years. Jewelry, I would have put in a box and never looked at it again.

DAY 15

MARCH 30, 2020

I slept a tad bit better last night. Still, I'm far from being well-rested. When I woke up, I went for a walk and headed to Juniper Valley Park. I'm not sure I'll ever get used to these deserted streets. There were no pedestrians and the schools I walked past were void of students and the windows were dark. Governor Cuomo's campaign to keep people from congregating in the parks is working. It's sad, though, that he had to go to such extreme measures. He said if people didn't heed his warnings, he was going to have de Blasio remove the hoops from the basketball courts. Sure enough, I walked by the courts, and the hoops were gone. The nets were also absent from the tennis courts.

Back home, I finally got a response to the email I sent last week to my son's principal. He is refusing to let us do a modified home-school curriculum. Instead, he sent us the paperwork to withdraw our son from school. In better times, homeschooling would be preferable. But with me not home and with Dad sick, it's not possible. As a result, we have no choice but to continue with things as they are.

The doctor called earlier today. Overall, Dad is improving—slightly. His blood pressure is up, but she explained that's probably because he is waking up and feeling agitated about being tied to the ventilator. Some people handle it better than others. Dad doesn't like it. I probably wouldn't like it either. It's a tricky balance between keeping him sedated enough but not sedating him too much. The doctor believes that most of Dad's problems stem more from the bacteria in his blood than the coronavirus. While he is slowly improving, he still has a long way to go. For at least another week (some patients need two), he will be on a ventilator. I'm disappointed that Dad will have a new team of doctors tomorrow. Apparently, they work on a rotating basis. I can only hope his new doctor is as good as the one he's had since Friday. I really like her, and I feel that Dad is safe with her.

I am not feeling well. The heat is on. I even asked my mom if I could raise it, because I'm cold. And I'm rarely cold. I have a headache, and I am coughing and sneezing. My body feels weak and tired. Maybe it's because I haven't been sleeping well. Staring at the screen is hurting my eyes, and the words are starting to blur. Perhaps I should step away for a while and, if not take a nap, at least rest.

Snapshot Rewind
1992: On Labor Day weekend, Mom and Dad drove me to New York University to move me into the dorm for my freshman year of college. As Mom was busy making my bed, Dad broke down the honor system for me; "4.0 is Summa Cum Laude; 3.8 is Magna Cum Laude; 3.5 is Cum Laude. Anything else is Cum Lousy. If you graduate Cum Lousy, you will have to pay me back your tuition."

Years later, he told me he was only kidding. But at the time, I believed him. Fear can be a great motivator. With a 3.51 GPA, I avoided graduating Cum Lousy.

DAY 16

MARCH 31, 2020

It is the middle of the night, and I can't sleep. It is my worst night thus far. Not only am I worried about Dad, I am also sick. I figured it would happen. But I had hoped it wouldn't happen so quickly or hit so hard. It started yesterday but intensified at night. I got so cold just before bed, I could not stop shivering. Mom put an extra blanket on my bed and still I shivered. I couldn't get warm. And then I was too hot. All night, I vacillated between sweating and shivering. But I don't have a fever; I've been checking periodically. The cough is what's worrying me most. I take a deep breath and I cough and cough and cough. My head is also screaming in pain. When I cough, it's like I'm getting smacked on the side of the head. I can't take Advil or Aleve because I've read that they may exacerbate the coronavirus—if that's what I have. When I sit up, it's as if I'm on the Tilt-A-Whirl at a carnival. The room spins rapidly around me, and I have to fight back the nausea. Finally, my muscles ache.

Now, I'm starting to worry about work. Before Dad got sick, I was struggling to transition to online teaching and to find the time to do it. Since Dad got sick, I've hardly been able to do anything. And now, forget it. How can I work when I feel like this? I'm so tired. My eyelids keep shutting. But once shut, sleep refuses to visit me. How can I grade essays or monitor discussion boards? If I were a full-time employee, I could take family leave to care for my mom or sick leave to take care of myself. I wouldn't have to worry about losing my job. As it is, the university expects me to do what they are paying me to do. I'm sure they want someone who can show up, but when I feel like crap, when I can't stand without falling down, when my head feels like it's in a game of whack-a-mole, how can I fulfill their expectations of me?

As expected, my boss called confirming my fear. I'm sick, my dad took a few steps backward today, and she doesn't see how I can continue teaching. She thinks it might be best if someone else takes over my classes. It sucks because in the midst of all this, not having a paycheck will really hurt. How do I pay medical bills without money? Or my loans? Or shop for food?

I am angry—about my job and Dad. It's not fair. He deserves so much better. But I am also jealous of everyone who can continue to go about their day as if it's business as usual. I'm jealous of people whose greatest frustration is trying to figure out how to teach a lesson on Zoom, of people whose biggest disappointment is not being able to go hang out at their favorite bar, of people whose greatest regret is not being able to go to church on Easter. Did the university not realize that this pandemic would reach its campus? Did they not realize that their faculty and students might be severely impacted by it on an intensely personal level? Surely the dean must be smart enough to comprehend the fact that this isn't happening only on the news. That people, real people, those who are loved and adored, are sick and dying. That educators are among the ill. That people who are living a nightmare day after day have more important things to think about and tend to than keeping up with lesson plans? At least I am smart enough to understand that we live in a capitalistic society and that decisions revolve not around compassion but around money. Keeping an adjunct professor who is too sick to work and too distracted about her father's condition to focus on discussion boards and grades is a poor business move. When money is at stake, there is no room for empathy.

Not long after I hung up with my boss, the doctor called. The news today is not as encouraging as it has been. Dad has water in his lungs that they are going to try to drain today. Plus, they had to increase his oxygen levels on the ventilator. The doctor is attributing his need for more oxygen to the fact that he is still fighting against being on the ventilator. His discomfort is hindering his improvement. I wish I could be there. If he could hear my voice, maybe he wouldn't be so upset. If he could hear my voice, he wouldn't think we abandoned him. At least I like the new doctor. He is as patient and personable as the other doctor had been. He made me feel like my dad is in competent, caring hands.

Early in the evening, my spouse texted me to say that my son carried his hamper upstairs to the washing machine. I can't be home to do his laundry, so he wants to help and do it himself. The text made me smile. I never would have thought that I could miss doing laundry. Not only did my son put his clothes in the washer, he also folded them. According to my spouse, "He folds better than I do." I think it's super sweet that he is trying to make this a little easier on me. Mom and I video chatted with him. He never has much to say, but his little cartoons of himself combined with his facial expressions continue to make us laugh. It's the only time we laugh all day.

Soon it will be time for bed. I feel worse, not better. I now have a fever. The last time I felt this horrible was in 2002 when I came home from Ecuador with malaria.

Snapshot Rewind
1980s: It's spring, and even though I haven't played softball in years, spring always takes me back to my childhood. And if the breeze is just right, and the smell of fresh-cut grass hits in a particular way, I feel as though I'm back on the field. For years, Dad

coached my little league team. He hated making phone calls, so every year, the task of calling players—this was before email made everything so much simpler—fell to me. "I'll happily coach, but you have to call," he told me. Oh, how I hated making those calls to set up uniform pick-ups and practices. I'd lift the wall rotary phone and my fingers would sweat, my head would spin. I was convinced I sounded like an idiot stuttering and sputtering through my lines. But I did it. I still hate making calls and I avoid it whenever I can. But I'm glad Dad coached my team. It always made me feel special, even though he was a great deal tougher on me than on everyone else.

DAY 17

APRIL 1, 2020

I got a few hours of sleep last night. But I'm not feeling any better. I've been able to keep my fever down with Tylenol, but my cough has gotten worse. So has my stomach, which is rebelling against everything I attempt to fill it with.

My boss called again. I am out of a job. They are passing my classes on to someone else, but my boss finagled a way to make sure I still get paid. I don't know exactly what she said or did, but I am grateful for this gift.

The conversation with the doctor did not go as well. They've managed to drain the water from Dad's lungs. However, his status on the ventilator hasn't changed. They had hoped to decrease the oxygen levels, but they haven't been able to. At least they haven't had to increase them either. Overall, the doctor said he is stable. We will take it. It is better than him going backward. Mostly, it's a waiting game, and I hate waiting. Especially now.

Since I hate waiting, and the doctors are unable to give us any definitive answers, I find myself clinging to little things, signs my friends send me that he will get better. Yesterday, one friend messaged me to ask how I was doing and to let me know that she was thinking of us and praying for Dad's recovery. She added, "As I am writing this, a little bit of sun shined brightly into my kitchen. I'm taking it as a sign ... All will be good." I hope she is right.

Bonnie—a close friend since we randomly met in a tourist agency years ago in Hanoi, Vietnam—has been sending my father reiki in an attempt to help him heal. Yesterday, while she was taking a walk on the beach and thinking about my father, she spotted a golf ball on the sand. "Does your dad golf?" she asked me in a message via Facebook.

"No," I messaged back. "However, he always enjoyed a game of mini-golf. Also, years ago, he used to collect golf balls he found on the beach out in Long Island. Sometimes, he and I would go out on his kayaks and paddle around near the golf course. We'd scan the water for balls that sank near the shoreline and grab them."

When I finished trying, three dots immediately appeared on her end, three dots that quickly turned into, "I'm going back to get the ball."

"You don't have to."

"I do." And she did. Later that evening, she went out to get the golf ball, and this morning, when I woke up, I was greeted with a picture and the message, "Here is your dad's first WA golf ball." It's like he really has to come home now. Or maybe I'm just desperate and need something to hold onto.

My son, despite being bored—I'm not home to rollerblade or bike with him—is behaving wonderfully. He's acting mature, cleaning his plates from the table after eating, cleaning his room, and logging into Google Classroom to take the initiative to do his schoolwork. This whole situation is crappy for him, as it is for the rest of us, but I'm glad he's not making things more complicated for my spouse. After dinner, my son and spouse took a walk—to go to the pharmacy for a peanut butter and chocolate egg—so that my son could get some fresh air and a bit of exercise. Because he is unlike any kid I've ever known, he had to get dressed up for the occasion. He wore a black sports jacket over a black tee shirt and his black fedora hat with a yellow flower tucked into the brim. Yellow, the color of hope. The color of optimism. The color of positivity.

Snapshot Rewind
1987–1988 school year: I did not get into St. Francis Prep High School. It wasn't because I wasn't smart enough, although that's what I believed at the time. It was because I didn't do well enough on the entrance exam. I have a deep aversion to standardized tests, an aversion that started when I was a kid. I have never tested well. In part, it's because I don't have the mental ability to concentrate when bored, and if I can see the sun through the window or hear birds chirping, forget it. It's also due to the fact that my brain doesn't work like other peoples', but I didn't discover that until years after the scarring began. Years of poor test scores enabled me to label myself as stupid, something I've never gotten over. Anyway, St. Francis Prep had a remarkable reputation, much better than the school I was beginning to think I would have to settle for. But my dad was not settling. He never settles. He knew I was capable of doing better than my test scores indicated, so he took a day off of work and went to the high school to speak to the "powers that be" in an attempt to plead my case. He brought my records from middle school to back up his testimony that I would indeed succeed if given the opportunity. My dad is very persuasive when he wants to be, and when I got home from school later that day, he was smiling, happy to inform me that I would indeed be attending SFP come the fall.

Not only did he get me into the school, he also managed to convince them that I deserved to be in math and science honors classes. He didn't have much luck in regard to English and history. My math test scores were less deplorable than my verbal ones. According to the school, since my verbal scores were so poor, I did not have the ability to excel in subjects that rely heavily on literacy skills—subjects such as literature and history. I think back on this often and laugh. I now hold an MA in history and an MFA in creative writing. I've had essays, book reviews, short stories, poetry, and a research paper published. I think it's safe to say that my reading and writing skills are pretty darn good. But I guarantee if I were to take a standardized test today, I'd still do poorly on the verbal section. In my opinion, test scores are like tea leaves: they want to predict the future, but they aren't always accurate.

DAY 18

APRIL 2, 2020

Last night, Mom and I watched Garth Brooks and Trisha Year-wood Live on CBS. They were raising money for doctors, nurses, and first responders who are poorly equipped to deal with this crisis. Medical staffs do not have the supplies they need to keep themselves safe as they scramble to try and save people. Mom saw the show advertised and said we should watch it. I was surprised. I enjoy country music. I saw Garth Brooks in concert years ago and have always liked Trisha Yearwood's songs. But Mom has never liked country music. I guess she needed something to take her mind off Dad. Music is good like that. Until it isn't. When Brooks sang a few lines from "If Tomorrow Never Comes," the tears were back. What if tomorrow doesn't come for Dad? What if my life with him is all in the past? What if we never see him again?

I woke up with another bout of nausea and a headache. I still have a cough, but I've found it's not as bad if I keep drinking water and tea. Not talking also helps. The more I talk, the worse it gets.

A few students—after I emailed to say I would no longer be teaching them—reached out to thank me for helping them become better writers and to tell me they are keeping me and my dad in their prayers. One student's email was particularly heartwarming. At a time when my world is unraveling, it's comforting to know that I've had a positive influence on someone's life:

Professor Jaeger,

Thank you for everything you've done this year from your stimulating discussions to helping revise essays. You made this semester enjoyable and really geared the work towards the student's needs. You let us choose our own topic and this motivated me to want to write a good paper because it was something I was interested in. I hoped we could've ended on a better note, however, I just wanted to take the time to tell you how greatly you impacted both my writing and my college experience thus far.

Your motivating attitude and strong willed mentality will push you to better days. I feel for you as well as everyone in your family during this time, but I have no doubt that you possess the abilities to overcome this obstacle. I hope you and your family the best! I just wanted you to know how much of a positive impact you have had on me because your hard work should not go unnoticed.

With warm regards,

R

There is no change today with Dad. The doctor had hoped that they would be able to start decreasing the oxygen levels, but Dad's lungs aren't cooperating. "It hurts not being able to be with him. I keep thinking if I could be there maybe he'd be more likely to improve," I told my spouse. "Like in the movies, when somehow the presence of a loved one revives the patient." But real life isn't the movies. Real life sometimes sucks. My cousins told me to focus on the fact that while he didn't improve, he didn't get worse either. That's got to mean something. But as I told them, I'm scared. I want him to come home. I want to hug him. I want my son to have more time with him—more love, more baseball games, more waffles, more movies, more everything.

They are movin Dad from Columbia Presbyterian to the Hospital for Special Surgery. The ICU in Columbia Presbyterian is getting too full, and Dad is not as bad as some of the new patients. Neither Mom nor I are happy about this. We trusted Columbia Presbyterian. It's one of the best hospitals in the country. But now, will Dad get what he needs to recover? Mom fears that they moved him because they don't think he's going to make it. I don't know what to think. On Friday, it had seemed there was no hope, but then his kidneys started to work, and his blood improved. I don't even know anything about this new hospital. I don't know if the doctors will work as hard or as efficiently. I feel so helpless. So lost. And I keep going back to the fact that I never hugged Dad when I dropped him off at the hospital. I never told him I loved him when he called to say he was going on the ventilator. At the time, I had no idea it would come to this. Or maybe I did, but I didn't want to believe it. I should have done more.

Mom and I played Scrabble as we do every night. It's the one thing I can do with her to help keep her mind off worrying about Dad. There are other games in the house, but none that either of us really care for. I went online to see if I could order Boggle, but the prices were so much higher than what we paid last year when we bought the game for my son. I guess with everyone sheltering in place, there is a high demand for games.

Snapshot Rewind
1980–1982: When I was in first and second grades, my parents enrolled me to take dance lessons—ballet and tap. All little girls want to be ballerinas. Right? No. I hated it. From the first moment I had to slip into that tight one-piece body thingy, I was miserable.

Every week, I dreaded getting on the bus with my mother and heading down Myrtle Avenue to my lessons. But I didn't tell my mother I hated it. Why? Because I didn't want to disappoint her and I sensed that she might be crushed if I told her the truth. Then one day, during my second year of taking lessons, parents were invited to watch the girls practice. I barely moved. I stood still, my face unable to disguise my misery. Later that night, Mom asked me if I wanted to quit. Even then I felt guilty. I knew how much it meant to my mother. As a child, she had always wanted dance lessons but her parents couldn't afford them. I felt like I was being mean by not liking something she had wanted. But I could no longer pretend to like something I dreaded. I nodded my head and so ended my dance career.

The following year, I asked my parents if I could join the basketball team at school. They said yes, and I was so much happier. Dad was, too. Years later, he grumbled about how much he hated the dance recitals. But basketball games—even before I could dribble or shoot properly—were so much more enjoyable for him. And me.

DAY 19

APRIL 3, 2020

It's been a week. Seven days since Mom woke me up with a phone call, and I took Dad to the hospital. It's been a very long week, by far the hardest of my life. But it has also passed in a blur. Blurred by time, or tears, or both. I've cried more in the last seven days than I ever have before. I don't know what to expect with the next phone call. My heart has stopped leaping when the phone rings. My legs no longer buckle. It's almost as if I've become numb. Afraid that the doctors won't be able to save him.

I feel better about Dad being in the Hospital for Special Surgery. It, too, has a great reputation. And once Mom calmed down a bit, she told me that she's been there. About a twelve years ago, she had knee replacement surgery and her room over looked the river. The doctor and staff were fantastic. I have no idea if Dad is also in a room that overlooks the river. It doesn't really matter. He's not in any condition to look out a window or enjoy a view, but Dad, like me, has always drawn strength from water.

Yesterday, the hospital told us the doctor would call every other day to give us an update. However, this morning, a doctor called and said he'd try to call us daily. Both Mom and I were very relieved. Our days are filled with waiting, hoping, and praying. If the doctor skipped a day of calling, we might fall into a panic. The doctor was spectacular. Like other doctors we have spoken to, he was kind and patient. He explained that even if Dad gets better, it won't happen any time soon. The average COVID-19 patient is on a ventilator for eleven to fourteen days. But that's only the average. Some are on longer. The recovery process is long and tedious. Therefore, it is entirely possible that Dad will go a few days without making any progress. He might also take a few steps backwards. The doctor emphasized, "That's no reason to lose hope. It's quite normal when a person is hospitalized for an extended time." Even if Dad has a bad day, that is no indication that Dad won't pull through. The doctor cautioned, "Look at the larger picture, not the individual steps." While there are signs that Dad's body is fighting the virus—which is great—the doctor still can't promise he'll come home.

My son is sad today. I talked to him this morning and told him that it is National Poetry Month. I suggested that he could write a poem, something to counter the boredom he has been wrestling. Usually, he enjoys writing poetry. I think it's his favorite genre—perhaps because poems are shorter than essays or short stories. After I spoke with him, he messaged me, "Mama, I really can't write a poem today." I asked why, and he explained he was feeling overwhelmed. Fridays, he said, are supposed to be catch-up days, days to finish the work he hadn't been able to complete during the week. But today, his teacher assigned new work. "Today we are doing more than usual." Plus, his grandfather is still in the hospital. Instead of looking forward to Disney and Universal, and a summer of fun activities with his grandfather, he's wondering if he'll ever see him again. To end our messaging conversation, he sent me a cartoon of a purple character crying, knees tucked up into his chest and a cloud dripping rain over his head. I wanted so badly to be able to go home and hug him, tell him everything would be okay. But what if it's not? And I can't go home, not until I kick this virus. Not until I don't have to worry about infecting my family. It sucks when the best thing you can do for your child is to stay away. I'm the mom who heals through kisses and cuddles. This is totally ripping me apart inside.

When I woke up this morning, I didn't feel too bad. My cough was mild, and I didn't have a fever. However, by mid-day, my cough had gotten worse, more persistent. And now I am burning up. For the first time, I have that foggy-headed feeling that usually accompanies illness. My eyes are glassy enough that reading has become a challenge. The words are blurring, and I can't wipe my eyes quickly enough.

Snapshot Rewind
1987: For part of our summer vacation, Mom and Dad took us to Washington, D.C. What I remember most clearly is our tour—or more specifically, a snapshot of the tour—of the Library of Congress. While standing outside, the tour guide explained that when the library was being built, the designers initially contemplated putting the faces of the world's greatest writers on the front door. He asked us who we thought might be part of such an elite cohort. Two women, who appeared to be friends, started rattling off the seemingly obvious answers: Shakespeare, Sophocles, Dante, Chaucer, etc. Meanwhile, my dad, speaking loudly as always, tossed out, "James Michener." The women rolled their eyes, a few people chuckled. In terms of writing, Michener is no Shakespeare. However, he is one of my dad's all-time favorite authors. In my adulthood, I've enjoyed his stories as well, mostly for the history they taught me.

DAY 20

APRIL 4, 2020

My symptoms are least problematic in the morning. I woke with a slight headache—that was it. Although extreme eye movement exacerbates the pain. If I look too sharply to the left or right, up or down, pain ricochets through my entire skull. Since I felt relatively well, I went out for a walk around the cemetery and then over to Juniper Valley Park. When my son was a toddler and my parents babysat, they would bring him to the playground there. Unlike Forest Park, which is closer, Juniper has a section of the playground fenced off for little ones so they don't get trampled by the bigger kids. It was often crowded, but my son enjoyed it. He especially enjoyed when Dad pushed him on the swing. In the warmer months, the ice cream truck would pull up, and the moment my son heard the music, he'd start running. Dad never says no to ice cream. He never says no to my son. My son would choose what he wanted based on the pictures pasted to the side of the truck, and then he'd eat it with a smile, ice cream dribbling down his chin. Today, the playground was quiet; no one was there. Hardly anyone was out at all. The gate was pulled shut, a lock holding it in place, and a red sign announced PLAYGROUND CLOSED.

Mom won't let me do my own laundry. I tried, but she got mad at me, insisting that she could do it. That she wanted to do it. I think what she wants is the distraction, something to do so that she can take a break from worrying about Dad. I wish the church was open. I understand why it isn't. At a time like this, even without Mass, the pews would be packed. But if Sacred Heart's doors were unlocked, I'd walk Mom over. I'd sit with her while she lit a candle and prayed the Rosary. Maybe that would ease her mind a bit. I have writing to give me comfort. Mom, I guess, is trying to find some level of solace in household chores. I'm trying to take care of her, but ultimately, I think it's taking care of me that's bringing her a little peace of mind.

It's Bonnie who calms me, or at least she tries to. I cried on the phone with her today because news from the doctor is upsetting. It doesn't look good. Through my tears, I told her, "Now it's his heart. Dad's heart isn't working as well as it should. The doctors are giving him medicine to help it pump more efficiently."

She reminded me of what I wrote yesterday, "Remember, the doctor said your Dad might take a few steps back now and then, but you shouldn't give up."

She's right, but the fact that his heart is failing scares the crap out of me. I'm so afraid that I'll never see him again. I can't imagine my son's life without his grandfather in it. Never has a man loved his grandchild as much as Dad loves his grandson. How is this happening to him? For ten years, I fought my father about spoiling him. I was upset when my son didn't act grateful enough, when he made demands. I should have just let it go. I should have just allowed Dad to enjoy spoiling him, making him happy. Because that is Dad's greatest pleasure—seeing his grandson excited.

The nurse in the hospital called us via FaceTime so that we could see Dad. He is sedated and obviously couldn't speak to me, but he got to hear my voice. He got to hear Mom's voice. Most importantly, I got to tell him, "I love you." It's not the same as saying it if he was conscious, but I still got to say it. I also told him that his grandson loves and misses him and that we all hope to have him home again.

I blame Trump for the fact that he isn't home. If our federal government had shut our borders sooner, prevented any sort of travel either into or out of the United States, things would be different. I'm fairly certain Mom and Dad got sick on their trip abroad—either on the cruise or the plane. Our government knew about the virus back in January. They knew it had reached our shores; they knew how deadly it is. But for months, they did nothing. My parents left in late February. If the government had shut our borders or at least issued a travel warning sooner, maybe my parents wouldn't have left. That's all Dad would have needed. A warning that travel was not advised—that it may not be safe—and he would have postponed his trip. He would have been bitter and angry, but he would have stayed home. And if he stayed home, he probably would not be sick. How many other Americans would be better off if we had a competent, honest president?

Today, my son was supposed to compete in another Taekwondo tournament. This one was supposed to be close to home in New Jersey. But like the others, it was canceled. Instead of being able to do something he enjoys, he is sitting at home completely distraught. "I tried talking to him about your father," my spouse told me when we spoke on the phone. "I tried to comfort him, but he told me to stop talking. When I didn't, he held a piece of fabric up to my face as if to physically block my words." I appreciate her effort, but my son loves his grandfather so much he can't bear to hear anything negative. He can't permit his mind to think that he might lose him. All he wants to do is sit on the couch, watch television, and forget bad things happen in real life. That not every story has a happy ending. To help redirect his mind from the sadness engulfing him, my spouse helped him make cookies. It helped for a bit, but he's back to being sulky.

I have no appetite. Neither does Mom. I am feeling empty and sad. I don't want to go to sleep. What if I wake up and tomorrow is worse? What if I wake up and he's gone?

Snapshot Rewind

1965-ish: Yes, that's way before I was born. But it's when Mom and Dad met. Mom was part of the 18 and Over Club at Sacred Heart. One Friday night, the club was hosting a social, and Mom baked cupcakes for the event. Wanting to make the cupcakes look pretty, she put a cherry on each one—stem included. My dad, not yet eighteen—he is nine months younger than my mother and never misses an opportunity to tell people he married an older woman—snuck into the party with his friends. The moment he saw my mom's cupcakes, he started to make fun of them, laughing loudly, obnoxiously. "Look at this," he announced, "whoever made these forgot to take the stems off the cherries." Mom fumed. She hated him. She thought he was childish and immature. Sometimes, she still thinks that, but obviously, he managed to weasel his way into her heart, despite his sometimes-childish ways.

DAY 21

This morning, I got an email that, under normal circumstances, would have made me happy. "The Write Life" section of *The Blue Nib*, a literary journal, published my travel essay, "The Monkey Temple." It is an excerpt from my unpublished memoir about backpacking through Nepal more than twenty years ago. "The Monkey Temple," describes my confusion and fear as I tried to navigate the unfamiliar streets of Kathmandu. It was my first time traveling alone, and my naïveté—in retrospect—was exasperating. The memoir goes on to detail my encounter with a twelve year old Nepalese boy and our experience trekking the Annapurna Circuit.

Before Dad got sick, the best part of publishing something was being able to post it on Facebook so that he would see it. So that he would read it and be proud of me. It's like, if I can't share it with him, then it isn't real. More than anything I wanted to do something in life that would make Dad proud. Yet, I feel as if I have spent forty-five years failing at everything.

The last few years, I have had some minor successes with my writing. I hoped that someday I'd find an interested agent, a publisher who thought my work worthy of publishing, and then I'd be able to give my book to Dad. I'd be able to say, "Look, Dad, I did it." I wanted to be a successful author so that he could hold my book in his hands and be happy. To know that his belief in me paid off. And now, that may never happen.

My morning walk brought me past the movie theater at Atlas Mall. The mall, like everywhere else in this city, was deserted. I didn't see one other person. Of course, the movie theater made me think of Dad since he loves movies. He and my son both love going to the movies, and when they go together, they seem to enjoy the movies more. My son always looks forward to his "Boys Day" outings with Grandpa. They make him feel special. And there are still so many movies they need to see together. Six weeks ago, my spouse suggested that we all go see *Call of the Wild*. My son had finished reading the novel, a prerequisite—as per my rule—for seeing the film, but my son didn't want to go. "I promised Grandpa," he said. "I'm going to see it with him." My spouse was disappointed, but she knew how important it was to my son. The book he had read was my dad's from when he was in high school. There is no way my son will watch the movie with anyone else.

After my walk, I drove to New Jersey to pick up more clothes. My spouse met me part of the way in a parking lot—near Garret Mountain—so that she and my son would have an excuse to get out of the condo. Since I'm sick, infected, I couldn't hug anyone or even get too close to my family. When I pulled in, my spouse jumped out of her car and tossed my things into my trunk. Then, we stood more than ten feet apart, trying to have a conversation. But what was there to say? "How's your mom holding up?" my spouse asked. I shrugged, "Falling apart. We both are." My son wouldn't even get out of the car. He looked crushed and barely waved at me. I wanted to hug him, and the fact that I couldn't, devastated me further.

Dad's condition continues to worsen. His heart is failing, and now his kidneys are starting to fail again. "I don't like to take hope away from families," the doctor told us, "but we need to start talking about the possibility of end-of-life care." In short, unless there is a miracle, Dad's not coming home. As the doctor talked, the room started to spin. I felt so incredibly nauseous I thought I might faint. I slipped to the floor, tucked my knees into my chest, and cried. Dad is the center of my world, my universe. Life without Dad looks so dark, so bleak, so barren. I think Mom is in shock or denial. Her face is stoic, but her eyes—soft and watery—convey her fear. She clings to her Rosary Beads, her lips constantly moving in silent prayer.

If there is a hell, this is it. I wish I could rewind the clock and prevent my parents from going on that cruise. I wish I could keep Dad close to me. Keep him safe so that he and his grandson could still have time to build more memories. Dad is only seventy-one, too young to leave us. I honestly thought we'd have more time with him. But I'll say this: the one thing I learned from Dad is that nothing in the world is more important than family. Nothing ever made him happier than being surrounded by all of us. So it really is shitty that he has to be alone now. It's such a cruel, awful twist of fate.

Mom and I Facetimed him and he looked worse than he did yesterday. When I said, "I love you," his mouth twitched. It was probably just a reflex, but I'd like to think it was him acknowledging that he heard me.

Snapshot Rewind
August 2014: Mom and Dad took my son to Disney World the summer he was four years old. It was probably the best week of his young life. My dad, as always, spoiled him, making his every dream a reality. On our second day there, we went to the Magic Kingdom. As we were getting ready to board the Peter Pan ride, I asked my son, "Who would you like to sit with?"

He looked at Grandpa, did a little dance, wiggling his hips side to side, and pointed—with both pointer fingers—to his grandfather and himself. "Boys with boys." Then, redirecting his fingers, he jabbed them at me and his grandmother, adding, "Girls with girls."

For the duration of the trip, he employed his little phrase, "Boys with boys; girls with girls," repeatedly. And my dad, basking in this very special role that his grandson had assigned to him, found himself doing things he swore for years he'd never do. Rollercoasters have never been my dad's favorite ride. In fact, he generally opts not to go on them. But Disney is Disney, and for that reason alone, certain life rules must be broken, at least on occasion. So, Dad, like the rest of us, got on line to ride the Seven Dwarfs' Mine Train. As fate would have it, my son got a seat at the very front—the best seat on any rollercoaster. Again I asked him, hoping he'd choose me. "Who would you like to sit with?" But alas, with an answer I expected—"Boys with boys"—he left me feeling slightly disappointed. But Dad in the front row of a rollercoaster? Never! However, to say no would have been to disappoint his grandson, and that he would never willingly do. He happily took a seat in the front, and with his arm around his grandson for the duration of the ride, he enjoyed every moment of it.

DAY 22

APRIL 6, 2020

Mom and Dad were supposed to be babysitting my son this week. It's Holy Week, and he is on spring break. I was supposed to be working. Wanting him to have fun and not have to sit at home or be bored accompanying me at work, I was going to bring him to Mom and Dad's. He was going to have a week of being spoiled. He and Dad were going to have "Boys Days" out and get McDonalds. They were going to watch movies and go to the beach. And now, instead of what should have been, we are living in an altered reality where I am in tears and my son is in denial.

All these years I've had it wrong. Life isn't made sweeter by traveling to more places or making more money or having security. Life is made sweeter by spending time with the people you love, the people who make you whole. I'm glad my son and I got to spend as much time with Dad as we did. I'm glad we have the memories. I'm glad my son got to experience such a special relationship with his grandfather.

My son called me this afternoon, a note of excitement in his voice. "I changed the lightbulb in the hallway, all by myself," he announced proudly. He was bored, so he figured he'd do something helpful. After my spouse finished teaching, she and my son took a walk to the pharmacy. There was a stuffed animal that my son wanted—a green bear. He called me up to ask if he could use his money to buy it. The poor kid has been so sad. How could I say no?

My cough is worse and my fever is higher—38.1 degrees Celsius. Mom called the hotline to see if I could get tested somewhere. A woman told her they aren't running tests anymore. So if they aren't testing, how are the numbers in New York going up? Why are celebrities still being tested? I asked this before, I'll ask it again. How rich, how famous do you have to be in this country for someone to care about you?

The news about Dad continues to be bad. He had a blood clot in his leg that traveled to his lungs. They are now giving him even more medicine to thin his blood. We keep hoping and praying for improvement, but Dad, despite fighting as hard as he can, keeps running into more problems. I continue to sink into sadness and despair. Mom asked the doctor if Dad would have been better off if we had brought him in sooner. The doctor said no, "With this virus, for some people, once it latches onto the body, there's no way to fight it." Even if I had brought Dad to the hospital when I first knew he was sick, I wouldn't have been able to save him.

It occurred to me, after a particularly touching message from a college friend, that many of you know my dad, and not just through my recent writing. You worked with him at New York Life. You've met him at track meets, basketball games, Boy Scout events (from my brother's time as a Boy Scout), and Taekwondo competitions. You've met him in essays I've published and through pictures on Facebook. You know my dad because he was always present in my life, in my brother's life, and then in my son's life. He is the type of dad and grandfather who shows up—all the time. You know him because he is always there for me, always active in everything I and my son do. He is in many ways the type of parent I aspire to be for my own son.

Snapshot Rewind

Fall 2010: Dad took Mom, my son, and me to the Bronx Zoo. He wanted to make sure his grandson got to experience everything possible. At only nine months old, my son could not yet walk, so he spent his time in the stroller and in Dad's arms. While we were visiting the tigers, my mom started talking to one of the volunteers. At some point, one of them mentioned Kopps Bakery on Metropolitan Avenue. When I was growing up, it was Dad's favorite bakery. We all loved the crumb cake. Every year for Christmas, Dad used to get the crumb cake for breakfast, and the sweet cinnamon flavor still permeates my memories of the holidays. But sometime in my early adulthood, it closed. Anyway, through the course of the conversation, the volunteer told my parents that he had Kopps's recipe for the crumb cake, and if Dad gave him his email address, he'd send it to him. Dad was eager to get the recipe, but he was skeptical the volunteer would actually follow through. Therefore, he was pleasantly surprised a couple of days later when the recipe appeared in his inbox.

Fast forward a few years. Now, my son loves Grandpa's crumb cake. Grandpa started making it for him every Thanksgiving and Christmas. Then one year, my son asked if he'd make it for Easter as well. Of course, Dad said yes. So that's what Dad should be doing right now. He should be home, making a crumb cake for his grandson.

DAY 23

APRIL 7, 2020

I dialed in to a Zoom Taekwondo lesson last night. I saw on Facebook that my instructor is going ahead with belt promotions and graduations in two weeks. I had not been taking classes via Zoom because our condo is too small. But Dad's last Christmas present to me was a year's tuition to study Taekwondo. I kind of feel I owe it to him to stay on track and move forward. While I haven't been participating in the Zoom classes, I was a bit of an overachiever before this pandemic shut everything down. Therefore, I have already learned many of the skills required for the cycle. Now, I'm going to see how much I can do—considering I am sick—so that I can hopefully get promoted to the next belt in mid-April.

Today has been my worst day. I stayed in New York to support Mom, but now she's the one taking care of me. When I woke up, I was so nauseous I ended up staying in bed much later than usual. I didn't want to get up, not until I felt I could stand without falling over. Then, I spent most of the day on the couch. My headache has gotten worse and my entire body hurts. A friend of mine, whose mom is a doctor, recommended that I take a washcloth, run it under hot water, squeeze it out, and then put it over my face. She said it would help keep my lungs moist. It helps my cough a little. When the cloth is over my nose, I can breathe a little more deeply, and I find the breathing doesn't trigger my cough as much. But, I'm still dizzy and I have the chills.

The doctor called earlier than usual today. There is no change in Dad, either for the better or for the worse. I guess after two days of bad news, we'll take it.

Snapshot Rewind

2016: Dad saw a meme on Facebook mocking the fact that kids are no longer learning how to write script in school. He was appalled, so much so that he loftily announced, "Civilized people write in cursive."

My son, who was six years old at the time, asked his grandfather what he meant by civilized. After Dad explained, "Civilized means smart and cultured," my son turned to me and said, "Mama, I have to be civilized. You have to teach me how to write in cursive." And so I did. That was the skill we worked on over the summer. It was also the summer my parents took him to Disney World a second time. When he got back from the trip, he was able to write an essay about his Disney adventures—in script. Grandpa was very proud of him.

DAY 24

APRIL 8, 2020

I forced myself to take a walk, to make my lungs expand and work a little harder, but everywhere I go, I'm surrounded by memories of Dad. I walk around Juniper Valley Park and I remember all the times he watched me play softball on the baseball fields in high school. When we first got Fireball—the golden retriever we all adored—we used to take her for walks in the park. Last fall, my son learned how to rollerblade, and Dad drove us over to the park so that my son could show off to his grandparents. That's the last time we were all there together. Mom and Dad sat on one of the benches while my son and I took off on our blades.

There is no change in Dad. The doctor seemed almost surprised that he isn't worse. That despite everything that's wrong with him, Dad is still fighting. Still wrestling with this awful disease. And even though the virus is winning, Dad's not giving up. He wants to come home. Ultimately, his body may not be strong enough to pull through, but he's giving this fight everything he has.

Mom and I spoke to him again today, and I thought about all the times my son cuddled up next to him in bed or on the couch to watch a movie or a television show. He needs that again. They both do.

Boggle arrived in the mail today. Bonnie read an earlier post where I mentioned it. She also sent us Rummikub, wanting to make sure Mom and I could play something other than Scrabble in an effort to keep our minds distracted.

Although my cough is better today—the warm washcloth over my face is working—I still have a fever and a headache. Plus, all food tastes funny. Water is especially awful. I can't even get it down, so I'm drinking tea. Lots and lots of tea.

Snapshot Rewind
August 1, 1988: Mom and Dad took us to Canada for summer vacation. Our first stop was Niagara Falls, and the plan was to leave at four o'clock in the morning. We always left early so that we could make the most of the day, so that we could get to our destination early enough to do something fun. I remember going to bed excited, eager to get on the road. I slept in my clothes—shorts and a T-shirt—so I could jump out of bed and get in the car without taking time to change. I even set my alarm a few minutes early to be the first one up, but my alarm never went off. Instead, Mom's hands gently shook me awake.

"Is it four o'clock already?" I asked, my eyes darting to my clock, wondering why my alarm was silent.

"No," Mom laughed. "It's just after one. Your father can't sleep; he's too excited. He decided we should leave now." And we did.

DAY 25

APRIL 9, 2020

In the last two weeks, I have lost ten pounds. Pants that used to fit me are falling off my hips. First, I couldn't eat because I was distraught about Dad. Now, my emotional response is compounded by the fact that food tastes terrible, and the foods I generally like to eat—greens, beans, and fruits—are wreaking havoc on my stomach. Plus, frequent bouts of nausea mean I'm constantly struggling to keep things down. The less I eat, the easier it is.

A friend of mine from high school, Brian, suggested I slice up ginger and boil it in water to make a ginger tea. It's a fantastic idea. Not only is my body not rejecting the ginger, it's alleviating much of my nausea.

Dad is still on a ventilator, and his lungs, according to the doctor, "continue to require a great deal of support," but his heart is functioning better. The doctors have been able to pull back on some of the medicine they were giving him.

Snapshot Rewind
Father's Day 2018: My son does not have a father. I believe this made his bond with his grandfather that much more extraordinary. In school, when students made crafts or other projects for their dads, my son always made something for my father. I don't believe he ever felt slighted, like he was missing something, because my dad was there to fill the space. On Father's Day weekend, we almost always drove out to Long Island to be with Dad. A few times,

I even pulled my son out of school on Friday so that we could have an extra day with him.

My son especially loves being with Dad for Father's Day because the Strawberry Festival in Mattituck is held that weekend. Vendors sell all sorts of goods from tee-shirts to jewelry and the smell of fried food permeates the air. We usually go on Saturday morning, and Dad buys my son a bracelet so he can go on an unlimited number of rides—the most exhilarating part of the festival. It was there that my son went on bumper cars for the first time. He wasn't tall enough to ride alone, so Dad—who always loved bumper cars— went with him.

Two years ago, a replica of the *Amistad* was out in Greenport. As soon as tickets went on sale, Dad bought them. It was one more experience he wanted his grandson to have. At eight, my son may have been too young to watch the movie, but we saw it with him anyway. We wanted him to understand the significance of the ship, the slave rebellion, and the trial that set the *Amistad* slaves free. On the boat, we—Dad, my son, and I—wore our matching *Star Wars* shirts that read, "The force is strong in my family," and my son sat next to his grandfather, learning history and enjoying the sea breeze on his face. This is why I love history, because from a young age, Dad found ways to make it real. It wasn't about dead people in textbooks. It was about places we could still visit today.

DAY 26

APRIL 10, 2020

Last night was the first night, in more than a week, that I didn't run a fever. This morning, my nausea wasn't as bad. But my taste-buds are still messed up. Those of you who know me, know that I start each day with espresso. I look forward it, drinking slowly to savor the flavor. Lately, however, it tastes disgusting. The only way I can get it down—to avoid a caffeine headache—is by replacing milk with lemon juice. That may seem odd, but Italians drink es-presso with a lemon peel, so it's not a completely novel combina-tion. Alcohol also tastes terrible, as does chocolate, and the thought of ice cream—which I generally love—makes me sick. Just about the only thing that doesn't taste bad is salad. In fact, balsamic vin-egar tastes even better than usual. There must be something in the acid—lemon juice and vinegar—that cuts through the ickiness of the virus.

My spouse doesn't have to teach today, so she wanted to do some-thing fun with our son. She was hoping to take him hiking, get him some exercise and fresh air. But Governor Murphy has closed all the state and county parks, making a fresh-air outing impossible. It's Good Friday. My son should be out on Long Island with my parents. Every other Good Friday of his life he has colored eggs with his grandmother, a tradition they started before he could even walk. "I feel bad for my grandson," Mom said, pausing between Rosary prayers. "It's a holiday, but it doesn't feel like one."

Dad is the same today as he was yesterday. His heart is functioning without the cardiac medicine, but his lungs are making no improvement. The ventilator remains at the highest setting. They've tried to pull back, but Dad's lungs aren't strong enough to do any work on their own. He has now been in the hospital, on the ventilator, for two weeks. At this point, the longer he stays on it, the harder it will be for him to come off of it. Sadly, he is showing no sign that he is about to turn a corner in the recovery process.

Feeling down, I took a walk. It was windy outside, and since there was a chance of rain in the forecast, I took an umbrella. It often rains on Good Friday. But this afternoon, it wasn't rain, it was snow and hail that whipped around me as I walked down 78th Avenue. It came down hard for about ten minutes, and then it abruptly stopped, leaving the sky clear.

Snapshot Rewind
April 10, 2009 (Good Friday): It was the day—eleven years ago today—my son was conceived. A very good Friday, indeed. Okay, maybe that's a bit TMI, but you've been on this journey with me for a while now. You know I put it all out there. Besides, you know my kid has two moms, so you know it happened in the very sterile environment of a doctor's office. It was our fifth attempt for me to get pregnant, and when we walked out of the doctor's office, my spouse and I were convinced that we'd have to try again. On that visit, I had only one follicle, unlike prior inseminations when I had at least two. That meant no chance of twins. The sperm count was also low. And we were supposed to show up for the insemination the day before—Holy Thursday—but my spouse and I had already missed so many days of work, we were afraid to take more time off. Looking at the math, the odds of success this time around were not in our favor. And so, two days later, when we sat down to Easter dinner with my parents, when my dad offered me wine, I didn't

turn it down. There seemed no point. I was most definitely not pregnant. Ha! But I was wrong. My spouse was wrong.

About three weeks later I went hiking. I drank water as I always do, but on that occasion I was parched and couldn't quench my thirst at all. Plus, I was ravenous. I ate a sandwich for lunch but it wasn't enough. I felt as if my hunger would never again be quelled. My whole body felt off. Therefore, when I got home, I took a pregnancy test, and sure enough, the little blue plus sign appeared. Blinking back my surprise, I opened the bathroom door to tell my spouse. She too was in shock and responded, "You've got to be fucking kidding me."

DAY 27

APRIL 11, 2020

I have now been fever-free for two days. But I continue to have a slight cough, and when I breathe in deeply, I can feel the virus nestled in my chest. I'm still sick. I'm still contagious, which means I will not be able to see my son on Easter. Easter has always been my favorite holiday. I'll take warm weather and an Easter egg hunt over Christmas any day. So it really sucks that Easter will be lonely and sad this year. True, I'll be with my mom, but Dad won't be home and I can't be with my kid. He's only ten, too young for me to have to skip out on a holiday with him. I wasn't supposed to miss a holiday with him until he went off to college. Everything about this damn virus is unfair. More than anything, I wish I was young enough to believe in fairy tales and happy endings. I want an Easter miracle. I want the virus to give up and leave my dad alone. I want his lungs to function again. I want my family to be whole.

My son talked my spouse into watching a horror movie last night—*Signs* with Mel Gibson. They were both terrified by the time it was over. According to my son, my spouse was more scared. But according to my spouse, it was my son who cuddled close and wanted to be held tight. My son has started adding food coloring to his lunchtime mac and cheese. He's stuck in the house, unable to do anything or go anywhere. I guess it's one way he can add a little variety—and color—to his life. This afternoon, my spouse went grocery shopping. When she came home, she noticed that my son had set the table for dinner. He even added salad bowls, but since neither of them eat salad, he filled the bowls with potato chips.

Mayor de Blasio has closed the New York City public schools for the remainder of the school year. I've been avoiding the news. I can't watch and hear about people dying, not when I'm trying so hard to hold onto hope. But every once in a while, some tidbit of news finds its way to me. I suspect New Jersey will be next. It's probably only a matter of days until the governor makes a similar announcement. My son hates learning remotely. My spouse isn't exactly a fan of teaching remotely. I think they are both hoping that school will open up before June. But with the numbers going up instead of down, I can't see how any government official could, in good faith, allow any sort of return to the way things once were. Not yet anyway.

Brian stopped by today to leave a bag of ginger on my mom's stoop. He read that it was helping and wanted to make sure I had enough to keep making tea. That was extremely kind and very sweet. It reminded me of when we were in high school and he used to meet me at the bus stop after school with a packet of peanut butter cups—my favorite.

Again, there is no change in Dad. He remains critically ill. Last night, a team of doctors and nurses flipped him into a prone position—a rather complicated procedure considering he's attached to the ventilator and oodles of other wires and tubes. Apparently, when a patient is on their stomach, it opens different parts of the lungs. They are hoping this change might somehow stimulate Dad's lungs to start working on their own.

I convinced Mom to take a walk today. Her feet and knees hurt, so we couldn't go far. But I think the fresh air was good for her. We had to be back home by three o'clock. The hospital said they would let us FaceTime Dad sometime after three. They are so busy, they can't give us an exact time. In fact, they are so busy, we waited the rest of the day, but the FaceTime call never came. I can't be angry—disappointed yes, but not mad. It must be chaos in the hospital as doctors and nurses fight to keep people alive. Still, I would've liked to have seen Dad, even briefly.

Mom isn't sleeping at all. Fear keeps her awake most nights. I'm not sure how she continues to function during the day.

Snapshot Rewind

Summers 1990s: Dad and I often played paddleball in the summer. We'd get up early before it got too hot and we'd head over to the paddleball courts in Riverhead. When I was younger, Dad almost always won. He had far better control of the ball, and one shot, low on the wall, that killed me every time. I was younger and scrappier. I could cover a greater distance, but when I hit the ball, it was often wild. Despite Dad's better control, in almost every game, he managed to accidentally whack me in the back of the head with the ball. It hurt, but it happened all the time, so I came to expect it and to joke about it. As I got older, I started to win more, but Dad still had that one lethal shot. After we played two, sometimes three, games, Dad took me out for breakfast—cinnamon rolls at the Tanger Mall. Then, sometime in the early 2000s, Dad announced that he was too old to keep playing. It was the end of an era and I was disappointed. We put the paddles away until last year when my son discovered them in my closet. He wanted to give the sport a try so Dad drove us into Riverhead and he and Mom watched while I taught my son how to play.

DAY 28

APRIL 12, 2020

This is by far the saddest holiday I've ever experienced. Easter morning is supposed to be happy. It's supposed to unfold like this: First, we are together in Mattituck. When my son wakes up, it's with a cry of delight that brings the rest of us out of our beds. On the table in the dining room are two Easter baskets—one from his moms and one from his grandparents, though he knows the Easter Bunny brought them both. Without asking, he dives into his chocolate, gobbling eggs and peanut butter cups until we remind him it's too early for so much sugar. Then, he opens his presents—this year it was supposed to be a couple of CDs—and goes in search of the Easter eggs. After all these years, you'd think he'd have all the hiding places memorized—the house is small—but he doesn't, and he still needs a hint or two. With the eggs collected, we sit down to breakfast. Before eating, we have our egg cracking contest. I think that's Dad's favorite part. We take turns smashing eggs against each other to see whose egg remains uncracked. Dad usually wins. I'm certain it's his technique, the way he holds the egg, his hand wrapped protectively around it. Once the eggs are all smashed, we have breakfast. The table is spread with bunny breads, Dad's home-made crumb cake, and eggs. When we finish, my son gets dressed, and I run outside to hide more presents from the Easter Bunny, presents his grandparents have bought him. This year, it was supposed to be money stuffed into plastic eggs, money he could take on vacation with him to shop for souvenirs. In the afternoon, we go to the beach and take a walk. For dinner Mom makes lamb. It's an Italian tradition, but since I don't eat lamb, there's a lasagna for me.

108

That's how Easter is supposed to play out. Instead, I'm in Queens with my mother, anxiously waiting for the doctor to call. Dad is in the hospital clinging precariously to life. And my son and spouse are in New Jersey, doing the best they can without me. The Easter Bunny brought my son a small basket with Kinder eggs, peanut butter cups, and foil bunnies with a note promising that there will be more when I come home. In essence, Easter is on hold until I am well enough to go home.

The doctor called later than usual today. It's been a hard day waiting for the call, and when it came, the news was disappointing. No Easter miracle for us. Dad had another blood clot overnight, and he is back on the heart medication. He's not giving up. He is still fighting. But his body is not cooperating.

After many tears, I convinced Mom to take a walk. We didn't go far, but it's good to get out of the house. We are now waiting for a FaceTime call, though it's beginning to look like they may be too busy again today. I understand. I really do, but at the same time, it's Easter. When the call finally comes, it's late, but just a few seconds of being able to say to Dad, "It's Easter. I wish you were here. We all really miss you," means a great deal. I just wish I knew definitely that he could hear me.

My son has been sad much of the day. I called to video chat with him, and he held his new stuffed animal—a bunny—up to the camera. "Look what I got," he smiled at me.

"Did the Easter Bunny bring you the bunny?" I asked.

He nodded and then his face fell. There is no use, for any of us, pretending to be happy. He was dressed up in a button-down shirt and a tie, wanting to make the day feel special. He even poured himself a glass of water and added a few drops of red food coloring to make it look like wine. But the day, despite our best efforts, feels empty. For dinner, my spouse is making London broil for herself and my son. Here, Mom is making baked ziti. It's Easter, but we have no cause to celebrate.

Snapshot Rewind
Memorial Day Weekend 2009: I drove out to Long Island by my-self to see my parents. I arrived late at night on Friday, and after I dropped my bag in my room, I reached for the picture I had brought with me. Heading into the living room, my chest bursting with excitement, I held out the ultrasound snapshot. "Mom, Dad," I announced, "I present to you, your grandchild." Dad's eyes glinted in the light as he stared down at the little dot that would someday grow into his grandson. Mom had tears in her eyes. I had made them wait long enough, but finally they were going to be grandparents.

DAY 29

The Easter Bunny stopped by Nonna and Grandpa's house last night to leave a basket of chocolate for my son. I sent him the picture this morning and he responded, "For me?" I chuckled. Who else would it be for? When I told him it was absolutely his, he typed, "Yayayayayayayayayayay." A glimmer of happiness in a sea of sadness.

Yesterday, since I had met the CDC guidelines of no longer being contagious, Mom asked me to go to the homemade chocolate store to buy candy for my son. "It's not fair that he had such a crappy holiday. His grandfather would want more for him. I'd feel better if I had a basket here for when he next visits."

While waiting for the doctor to call, Mom and I played three hours of Rummikub. It's after one. He never calls this late. Our anxiety is mounting. We fear the worst. This waiting is painful. It's impossible to do anything. We can't even play anymore. I've taken to pacing in the kitchen and staring out the window, at the rain beating down and the wind knocking around the tree branches.

The doctor's words left of us reeling, "Gary is a strong man. With everything he has already endured, I'm surprised he's still alive." He then when on to say that despite their best efforts, they are at a loss. They don't know what else to try to get Dad's lungs working. In short, the doctor doesn't think Dad will make it. "Keep praying," he encouraged, because at the moment, science is tapped out. They've tried a few experimental drugs, and none of them worked.

Other drugs, such as Remdesivir, they can't try because of Dad's secondary infection—caused by the bacteria in his blood. It doesn't make sense. If the situation is desperate, how could giving him Remdisivir be worse than doing nothing? If he might die anyway, why play it cautiously with a drug that might turn things around? But I'm not a doctor, just a daughter not yet ready to give up, not yet willing to say goodbye. It's devastating and discouraging when even the doctors don't know what else to do. I want him to come home so badly, but I feel so powerless. All I can do is pray and meditate and hope. But, it's not enough.

I didn't do much of anything today. I feel numb.

Snapshot Rewind
Spring, sometime in the mid-to-late 1970s: I was little, probably still a toddler since I had not yet started school. It was the weekend, and Mom needed to clean the house. She asked Dad to please take me outside, to entertain me so she could get some housework done. Dad looked at me and said, "But I don't know how to play with a girl." Mom wasn't having it. She told him to take me to the store, buy me a bat, and teach me how to play baseball. Dad complied, and as he was getting me into the car, Mom added, "Just make sure you don't buy her a blue bat." But hey, this was the 1970s and everything was gendered back then. Of course bats only came in one color, so Mom was a bit dismayed when we got home and I was carrying a blue bat. But the color didn't matter. Not to me. What mattered is that Dad set me up by the garage, properly positioned my hands on the bat, and taught me how to swing. Softly, he pitched until I learned to make contact. That afternoon, a love of baseball was born. Over the years, Dad and I spent countless hours playing baseball or just having a catch.

DAY 30

This morning, while I was out walking, I called my spouse. "What I really want for our anniversary is for Dad's lungs to start working again."

"When's our anniversary?" she asked, as if surprised we have one.

"Ummmmm ... tomorrow." That's the whole reason we got married on Tax Day, so we wouldn't forget. So I wouldn't forget. Our first year together, I forgot to wish her a happy birthday. Her birthday is two days before mine, it should have been easy to remember. She was mad, justifiably so. I didn't think she'd ever forgive me—I'm still not certain she did. When we were picking a date to get married, she suggested we go with a day that we couldn't forget. Not a holiday, but a date that would be tossed around enough in the news that it would be impossible to forget. For that reason, we settled on April 15.

"Really? Ugh. I don't know what day it is anymore," she sighed into the phone. I can't be angry. All days are bleeding into each other. There's no reason to keep them separated. "I even missed my dad's birthday. I completely forgot until late at night," she explained, "when I was at the supermarket looking at expiration dates. But taxes aren't due, right?"

Right! Our plan exploded around us like everything else. Yes, Tax Day is postponed, which is why no one is talking about it. Which is why we had no subtle—or not so subtle—reminders. The media has bigger, more important things to report. My spouse doesn't have to scramble to get our taxes done. But, Dad's lungs working would be an incredible anniversary present. If I got that, I'd never ask for anything else.

Mom is angry, when she isn't sad. She told me, "If your father dies, I'm going to go down to the local Republican office and I'm going to stand outside with a sign that says DONALD TRUMP AND THE REPUBLICANS KILLED MY HUSBAND." I chuckled, because I'd love to see that, Mom holding a political sign. Trump knew about the coronavirus back in November. By January, he was aware that it was here, and he did nothing to stop the spread, nothing to warn the American people. He had the intel but neglected to act on it. He should have advised people not to travel. My parents—in late February—should have been warned not to leave the country. If we had a competent president, Dad probably wouldn't be dying.

And Daddy is dying. Not one doctor on his team sees an optimistic outcome. An x-ray of his chest shows that his pneumonia is worse. There is nothing they can do to save him. Mom is devastated. My son is distraught. And I have no words for how upset and sad I am. Bonnie called and cried with me. There is nothing else to do but cry. Dad meant the world to me, and I'm not ready to face the world without him. It's not fair. He's too young to die.

We FaceTimed Dad to say goodbye. I cried through the call. "I love you," I told him for the very last time, and then words spilled out in a chaotic monologue because he couldn't respond. "Thank you for being the best Dad a kid could have. Thank you for being an even better grandfather. And thank you for putting up a good fight. I want you to come home. I want to see you again, but if it's too hard, if you can't fight anymore, it's okay. You can let go. We'll be okay. We'll miss you, a lot, but at least we'll have wonderful memories of you for the rest of our lives." Thanks to my cousin's suggestion, my son made a video telling his grandfather he loves him. I was able to play it for Dad so that he could hear his grandson's voice one last time.

They are taking Dad off the ventilator. He is going to die. Hope is lost. A priest administered Last Rites virtually since Dad couldn't have visitors. More than anything, I wish I could be there with him to let him know he isn't alone. My pain is great, but I know my son is feeling even worse. I just wish Dad had more time with his grandson. He wanted so badly to take him to Disney one more time. He wanted to see him bridge over into Boy Scouts next year. He wanted to see him compete in districts for Taekwondo. And he wanted to attend his college graduation. There are so many regrets, but there are also so many beautiful memories. At least they had ten years to love each other. Ten years of riches.

At four-twenty the doctor called for the final time. Daddy died at 4:14 p.m. on 4/14. When I was a child, I considered four to be my lucky number. I wore number four for years playing both softball and basketball. One year, during college, I wanted number four for one of my summer leagues, but my friend beat me to it. Since it was a summer league, a league to play in just for fun, they let me be negative four. I played shortstop. My friend played second. Standing together, we were zero, which won us many laughs. Then I moved to Korea, where I learned four was the unluckiest number of all. In Asia, they regard number four the way we regard thirteen. Four is unlucky because, in Chinese, the pronunciation of the number is similar to the pronunciation of "death." When a Korean friend first explained this to me, I laughed. It seemed so silly. How could a number, especially four, be unlucky? But now, what else could four possibly represent? Daddy died in the fourth hour, in the afternoon of the fourth month.

It's so cliché, but I am heartbroken that he is dead. Telling my son was the hardest thing I've ever done. His tears spoke volumes. He loved his grandfather dearly, and his death has left a gaping hole in my son's life. This is not the ending I wanted, but I am grateful for your prayers, your love, and your support. Thank you!

Snapshot Rewind
1969: Mom was part of the drama club down at Sacred Heart. She didn't act. She's too shy and doesn't like being the center of attention. Instead, she was part of the set design team. One evening, she was helping to paint the set when my dad walked in. He stood awkwardly in the back of the gym and watched as Mom and others painted. Finally, an older woman turned to Mom and said, "You should go." My mom, completely oblivious, started to protest, so the woman added, "Gary isn't here for me." Mom smiled and put her paint supplies away. Dad offered to walk her to the bus stop. But Dad was nervous, so it wasn't until the bus pulled up and Mom got on that he plucked up the courage to ask her out on a date. As the door closed between them, Mom smiled, nodded, and said, "Yes."

DAY 31

APRIL 15, 2020

It is the middle of the night—three-seventeen to be exact—and I can't sleep. I took medicine before bed, but it isn't helping. Lying in bed, I can't stop thinking about Dad. A movie scroll of memories plays continuously in my head, and I am full of sorrow that I will never again hug or be hugged by the man who loved me so deeply for forty-five years. It isn't real. This was supposed to be a story about recovery, not one about grief.

Dad often joked that he wouldn't read women authors. He didn't like women writers because he found their language to be "too flowery." There were only three women authors he enjoyed: Sue Grafton, Colleen McCullough who wrote *The Thorn Birds*—he loved that novel—and a third whose name I don't recall. I often kidded with him that even if I ever managed to publish a book, he'd never read it because it would have been written by a woman. But I know that isn't true. He'd have been the first person to buy it. However, knowing how Dad felt about female writers, there is a great deal of irony in that I am the one telling his story, writing this memoir.

I won't use euphemisms for Dad. He died. He didn't pass. He isn't lost. And he's not gone. He is dead. I won't use euphemisms because Dad hated them. Whenever Dad heard someone say they lost someone, he muttered to me, "Well they should go look for them." I wish Dad was only lost because then I would go searching for him. I'd search the world over until I found him. As it is, I have to learn how to live without him, and with the way I've been crying and falling to pieces, I haven't exactly been a pillar of support for Mom. I hug her when she cries, and then we cry together. There have been so many tears.

Because this pandemic has caused everything to shut down, we can't have a funeral or a Mass for Dad. Just one more aspect of this whole miserable ordeal that isn't fair. We won't be able to see him one last time; we won't be able to say goodbye. Mom said he wanted to be cremated, so she will honor his wishes. My son, expecting a wake and a funeral, asked my spouse if he'd see Grandpa one last time. On the phone she told me, "He wanted to know if he could put one of his Lego sets in the coffin with your father." The sentiment made me cry—again. My dad and my son spent countless hours together doing Legos, and it's touching that my son wanted those memories to be with Dad in some tangible form forever.

Last night, after dinner, I opened Dad's liquor cabinet, and instead of my usual Black Russian, I made myself a Manhattan. I'd never had one before, but it was Dad's favorite drink. It only seemed appropriate that I should have one in honor of Dad. As I reached for the Maker's Mark and the vermouth, Mom asked, "Do you even know how to make a Manhattan?" With a sad smile, I answered, "Of course. Remember, I occasionally made them for Dad."

While I had my drink, Mom and I watched *Law and Order: SVU*. During the show, Dad's iPad pinged. I looked to see why, and there was a message from my son, "Love you Grandpa." This morning, I came home from my walk to find Mom crying. "Let me show you this," she said, as she led me through the door. She picked up Dad's iPad and there was another message from my son, "Good morning Grandpa." He's processing his grief by still trying to communicate with the person he loved most. Two years ago, Mom and

Dad bought him an iPad for his birthday. The best part of having it was that he could send messages back and forth to Grandpa. Mostly, he sent GIFs and little cartoon characters. Dad loved getting those messages. He loved knowing that his grandson was thinking of him. The little Doodle Jump guy was one of their favorites.

Today is my wedding anniversary. Fifteen years ago, my spouse and I traveled up to Toronto to get married. Queer marriage was not yet legal in the United States—only in Massachusetts, but you had to be a resident of the state—so we had no choice but to cross the border. Mom came and was one of our witnesses. Dad couldn't come. Fireball, our dog, was old and sick, and he didn't want to leave her alone. Though I was disappointed Daddy couldn't be there, I understood. He told Mom to take us out for dinner to celebrate after the civil ceremony, so he was there in spirit.

This probably sounds corny, but I am taking comfort in knowing that Dad has been reunited with Fireball. If there is a heaven, she was there waiting for him, and when he arrived, she greeted him with a wagging tail and a glint of excitement in her eyes. Dad is with her now, and though he is sad he had to leave us, she will keep him company until we see him again.

This morning, my spouse and son drove to New York. According to the CDC website, I'm not contagious. Still, I had originally wanted to wait a few days before seeing them. However, after Dad died, I needed to be with my son. Perhaps it was selfish of me, but I thought it best if we could grieve together—me, my son, and Mom. When they arrived, my son's eyes were red. I knew he had been crying. I also knew how incredibly hard it would be for him to walk into this house for the very first time without Grandpa to greet him. I knew because I remember the first time I walked into my grandparents' house without my grandmother being there. I, too, was ten. And it felt so unbelievably empty. Her presence was everywhere, but she was nowhere. The house felt too big. Too hollow. And I knew it would hit my son like a wave in the ocean, knocking him down and completely disorienting him.

When my son arrived, I asked him if he was hungry. If he wanted breakfast. He didn't answer. Instead, he marched into the kitchen, demanded Dad's apron, and once it was wrapped around him, he commenced making pancakes. Dad should have been here to make breakfast for my son. He loved making breakfast for his grandson, it was one of his greatest pleasures, but since he isn't here, my son took charge. He wouldn't let me cook. He wanted to be like Grandpa, and he made Mickey Mouse pancakes because that's what Dad always made for him. But as he poured the final batter into the frying pan, he pulled up the stool, sat down, pulled his knees into his chest, dropped his head, and cried. I quickly enveloped him in a hug. "Mama," he said, "I feel really bad. I should have texted Grandpa more. I should have sent him more messages." I tried to comfort him. I told him that Grandpa loved him and that he enjoyed the messages he did send. "But Mama, you were right. I should have been more grateful. I should have said thank you more. I should have been happy with what Grandpa gave me."

I was crying with him. "Oh, honey, Grandpa didn't need you to say thank you. Your happiness, your smiles were all he needed. He loved you. All he wanted was for you to be happy."

He picked up his head, tears streaking down his cheeks. "But Mama, he really wanted to see his cousins Anna and Tani. And I'm really sad that he is sad, that he died before he could see them. It's not fair." No, it absolutely isn't fair. How many times have I said those same words? None of this is fair. Dad deserved so much more.

"Yes," I agreed with him. "But let's be happy for all the things Grandpa did get to do. Let's remember all the happy times you and I had with him. Let's celebrate the memories we have." He collapsed into my arms and I pulled the pancakes off the stove and held him while we cried.

Snapshot Rewind

Fall 2004: When my spouse proposed to me, I was living with my parents. One afternoon, she came over for dinner and we told my parents that we were going to get married. Dad looked at me with a big smile and said, "Does this mean you're finally moving out?" But then his eyes shifted to my spouse and he added, "Or does it mean you're moving in?" We all chuckled. I had moved in and out so many times it started to seem like I was a boomerang. (Come to think of it, even after my son was born, I was here visiting an awful lot. They never really did get rid of me.) After our laughter settled down, Dad hugged me and said, "I really just need to know how I'm supposed to address an envelope." I was marrying a woman, but it didn't matter. Dad handled that like he handled everything—with a touch of humor.

DAY 32

APRIL 16, 2020

Daddy loved the beach. It was his favorite place. For years he had basal cell skin cancer. It was the "good" cancer, meaning it wasn't going to kill him. But he had growths all over his body that had to be removed yearly. Once, when my son was little, maybe five or six, Dad had a large swath of skin on his back removed. Since pig skin is the closest to human skin, the doctor put pig skin on the wound to help it heal. When Dad told this to me and my son one morning during a FaceTime call, my son started to cry. "Oh no, Grandpa. Does that mean you're going to turn into a pig?" No, we assured him. Definitely not. But Dad probably should have avoided the sun. However, not going to the beach in the summer was not something he would consider. During the warm months, he lived at the bay out on Long Island. When he retired, as a present, I bought him a swim shirt. He always swore he wouldn't wear one because they were uncomfortable and he'd get cold in the water quicker. But I also knew that if I bought him the shirt, he'd wear it. And he did. He also always sat under an umbrella to keep the sun off his skin as much as possible.

Many of my memories of Dad, and many of my son's memories of his grandfather, are of us at the beach—swimming, playing with the beach paddles, kayaking, playing running bases, eating ice cream, Dad and I tossing my son back and forth in the water when he was a toddler. When my spouse and I were too poor to afford a summer vacation, it didn't matter because my son could spend countless days with his grandparents at the beach in Mattituck. It was the best vacation a young kid could have. But here is what really bothers me: I can't recall the last time I was there with Dad. We spent so much time at Veteran's Beach, but I have no specific memory of our last day. When the previous summer ended, I told my son we'd be back. Every year it was the same, and I had no reason, back in September, to think differently. But last year, we carried our belongings up to Dad's car one final time, not knowing we'd never do that again. Never again will we take another walk on the sand, my son holding his grandfather's hand. We'll never watch another sunset together. And my son and his grandfather will never again leave Mom and me behind to go off to McDonald's for a boys' lunch outing. Summers, as I knew them, are over.

Yesterday, Mom was talking about how she wants to have a Mass and a memorial service for Dad once the pandemic passes. I immediately said I'd write the eulogy, but as I was talking, my son yelled at me, "Did you ever think that maybe I'd want to write the eulogy? Don't you think I'd want to tell stories about *my grandfather?*" I had tried to get him to write a letter to his grandfather. I'd tried to get him to write down his memories as I have been doing, but he wanted no part of it. As soon as Grandpa ended up in the hospital, he refused to write. How was I supposed to know he'd want to write the eulogy? Not wanting to argue, I took him in my arms, and hugged him. "I'm sorry. You're right. I should have asked you. But we can both write one," I promised, knowing that there could never be enough words said about the man we loved so dearly.

My son is angry about more than the eulogy. I've never seen him so pissed off. And he is taking it out on me. We went for a walk— Mom, my son, and I. I've been trying to get Mom to walk every day. I think the exercise is important. But my son complained every moment we were out. "You don't care about me," he accused. "You're not giving me enough attention. Stop talking to Nonna and talk to me." I know he is lashing out because he misses his grandfather. His grandfather always gave him his complete attention, and when he was here, nothing else mattered. Dad always knew the right thing to say to my son. He always found a way to make everything better.

Once my son calmed down, he spent most of the day doing jigsaw puzzles—puzzles he uncovered in Mom's basement closet. He put together a 100-piece puzzle all by himself and a 300-piece puzzle with a little help from Mom. I didn't force him to do schoolwork. I couldn't. We all needed a break from responsibility, from thinking about anything beyond our pain. If school were still in session and he could have gone to an actual physical place, surrounded by friends, I wouldn't have kept him home. But it didn't seem fair to make him work in a place where he'd be completely surrounded by memories

As I deal with Dad's death, I'm tired of hearing people talk about a return to normalcy. In fact, when I hear the phrase, I get angry. For me, for my son, for my mother, there won't be a return to anything. The world we loved, the world in which we lived, the man that made us happy, is dead. When the pandemic passes, I will need to orientate myself to a new existence. When I need parenting advice, I can no longer call my dad. When I'm miserable in New Jersey, I may not be able to escape to Long Island. When I feel lost, I can't call Dad to find my way. And when I have something to celebrate, he won't be there to celebrate with me. The post-pandemic world will be void of the love I took for granted, the love I thought would always be there. I'm not ready for the world to open up because I may never get used to him not being here.

Snapshot Rewind
Winter, sometime in the early 1980s: I have always loved snow. As a child, I remember Mom and Dad taking my brother and me up

to Forest Park to go sledding. We'd sneak through a hole in the fence and onto the golf course. When I was little, Dad would lay down on our Flexible Flyer, and I'd lay down on his back, wrapping my arms around his neck. He'd push off with his hands, and together we'd go tearing down the hill, the wind and snow whipping our faces. I felt like I was flying.

DAY 33

APRIL 17, 2020

A FedEx package arrived this morning from the hospital with Dad's belongings. Opening it up ushered in another round of tears. When I drove him to the hospital, I expected him to come home. Rummaging through his backpack and finding a change of clothes, it was apparent he, too, expected to come home. It was like the suitcase he packed for vacation, the suitcase he didn't live long enough to unpack. His life, his story, was not supposed to end the way it did. And I'm angry at myself for being a coward. When I saw how bad he looked, I should have flown into his arms and given him a hug. But fear of the virus—a virus I ended up catching anyway—kept me away. I will always regret that act of cowardice. When Dad needed a hug most, I didn't give it to him.

I'm still not sleeping well. I wake up in the middle of the night to go to the bathroom and then I can't fall back to sleep. I lie in bed thinking about Dad, replaying memories, and reflecting on all the things we'll never get to do, as well as all the experiences that will carry on without Dad.

Years ago, at my baby shower, a former student, now friend, gave me a journal. In it, she included a beautiful note:

Elizabeth & Kati,

I searched tirelessly to find the perfect storybook for you to share with your sweet little baby boy. As I rummaged through aisles and

126

rows of books, I realized that no story I chose could be more magical than the one you both could create for your son. May you fill the pages of this journal with memories and stories that will delight and inspire him, as well as bring the three of you that much closer.

With love always,
Jocelyn

I am now on my sixth journal for my son. Thanks to Jocelyn—for I'm not certain I'd have thought to keep a journal had it not been for her gift—I've kept a diligent record of all the things we've done as a family. Often, I've commented to my spouse that the journal was the best present I got at the shower. While my son has long since outgrown all the other books, toys, and clothes, I'm still writing his story. Since Dad died, the journal has suddenly become even more valuable. Pictures are incredible for walks through the past and for reminiscing about what once was, but the written word is even more powerful. Within the pages of my son's journals is a record of all the amazing experiences he got to share with his grandfather. And while there won't be any more, my son is immensely lucky to have had my dad for as long as he did. Someday, when he is older, he'll be able to read the journals and relive those special times—even the ones he might have been too young to remember.

But that is still in the future. In the moment, right now, he is having a hard time. He's too young to be dealing with the awful, unfair, and untimely death of his grandfather. And he's taking it out on me. I tried to ease him back into doing some schoolwork today and he exploded into a tantrum. I know he's in pain, but it feels like he's trying to punish me. As if I am somehow to blame, and maybe I am. "I'm angry I didn't get to see him," he shouted at me. "That I didn't get to talk to him. The last time I saw him was in

January. He was alive for two months after that, but you didn't take me to see him. Not once," the accusations flew out of his mouth and ripped me apart. But what was I supposed to do. When his grandparents returned from Patagonia, I didn't visit because I was afraid my son might be an asymptomatic carrier of the virus— even back then I was listening to and heeding the warnings—and I didn't want him to possibly infect his grandparents. In retrospect, I wish we had driven to New York to see them when they landed. But if we had, perhaps I would be feeling as if we had killed him. As if Dad's death was my fault. And that would be worse.

As my son stormed up the stairs, away from me, Mom got off the phone with the funeral home. Dad will probably be cremated sometime next week, but they are sending his body to Connecticut. Take a moment and think about that. He died three days ago and it will be another week before the cremation. Plus, they have to send him across state lines because there is too much of a backlog here in New York. And yet, somehow on social media people are calling this virus a hoax. Anyone who believes that should travel to New York and see the corpses piling up, the freezer trucks full of bodies because there's nowhere else to put them. Luckily, Dad died in a good hospital and mom is dealing with a funeral home our family has done business with before, so Dad's body is in a morgue, not a truck. But not everyone is so fortunate, and it appalls me that Trump will not speak out against the stupidity, the claims that the virus isn't real, that it isn't deadly, that it isn't a major health concern.

However, I am relieved that Dad wanted to be cremated instead of buried because in the excitement—ten years ago—of naming my son after him, it never occurred to me that someday my young son might have to read his own name on a headstone. Now, without a burial, I won't have to worry about that on top of the anger and sadness my son is already trying to process.

Bonnie texted me asking a simple question, "How are you?" My answer, "Not well. I may never recover emotionally. It's not a normal death." I've been so concerned with my mom and my son that I didn't stop to think about me. I've been running on adrenaline and pouring my emotions out into my writing. It's helped, but the truth is I am not doing well. Sure, I expected my parents to die at some point, but not like this. My own life seems to be spinning wildly out of control. I need to be here for my mother. I want to be here for my son, but maybe it's too much for him right now being in his grandfather's house. Which means, once again, I have to choose between my mother and my son. And my mother probably needs me more because she has no one else. But how can I take care of everyone else when I'm not doing well myself? How can I be there for my son, when I'm falling to pieces?

If there wasn't a pandemic, I'd be able to go out. I'd be able to make plans to run away for a while—with my family. I'd be forced to show up for work. I'd be able to see people at Taekwondo. I'd be getting ready to meet with my writing friends at the end of the month. But the pandemic is still raging. People are still dying. And so this shelter in place has me trapped inside my grief.

This is why I am grateful for Bonnie. Who knew, when we randomly met fourteen years ago—on Dad's Birthday—in a travel agency in Hanoi, Viet Nam, that she would be such a comfort to me in my darkest hours. In the last month, she has walked with me through this whole miserable experience. If it wasn't for her, I don't think I'd be standing at the moment. She even messaged my son trying absorb some of his pain. When I needed a friend most, she was there—completely. How bizarre that we first met on Dad's birthday and that she was there to hug me—virtually and spiritually—on the day he died.

Snapshot Rewind
Spring 2010: My son was born with a flat head. It looked almost as if one-third of his head was missing. "An alien," is what my spouse said he looked like. In order to correct it, to round out his head, he had to wear a helmet. But helmets weren't cheap, and of course insurance didn't cover it. We couldn't afford the helmet. I had lost my job—on the record because of budget cuts, but in reality because the administration didn't like the fact that I was out to my students—when I was pregnant, and we were surviving on a single teacher's salary. So Dad, as always, said not to worry about the cost, he would cover it. He wanted the best for his grandson. And when my son needed a second helmet, he—and my mother-in-law—paid for that one as well. Daddy always took care of us.

DAY 34

APRIL 18, 2020

Last night, after I had gone to bed, my son came into my room and curled his body into my arms. He didn't say anything; he just snuggled as close as he could. And I held him. I'm not sure who needed whose comfort more. He fell asleep in my arms. When I woke up in the middle of the night, smothered by memories and regret, I still couldn't fall back to sleep, but hugging my son made me feel less alone.

This morning, neither one of us could get up. Every morning since Dad died, I feel like I'm weighted down by a lead blanket. Who knew absence and emptiness could feel so heavy?

There are times I find myself standing at the front window, staring at the walkway. In those moments, I am a child again waiting for Dad to come home from work. Waiting for him to open the door, drop his briefcase by the wall next to the stairs, and pull me into a hug. For a split second, he isn't dead, and if I train my eyes just so on the street, I might see him.

My son and I came home to New Jersey this afternoon. I won't leave my mom home alone long. I'll go back tomorrow. But I thought my son and I needed some time together. When we got home, a postcard was waiting for him, a postcard that came in the mail yesterday. The postcard was written in Dad's handwriting and mailed over a month ago.

Dear Gary,

We just arrived in Chile and haven't gotten to the boat yet. Looking forward to a great time.

Love,
Nonna & Grandpa

He had no idea that the great time he was looking forward to would kill him. No idea that less than a month after he had written that, he'd end up in the hospital. Dad had been so excited about that trip. He couldn't wait to go away. In his retirement, two things gave him a great deal of pleasure: spending time with his grandson and traveling. It's unfair that doing one cut his time short with the other. Every year, he and my mom took a Viking cruise. They traveled the world, seeing beautiful and historical sites and spending time together. Sadly, my mother is now left with bad memories of that last trip. Her last vacation with her husband ended in unimaginable tragedy. "We had lots of fun together," she told me, "but I will always look back on that trip with sadness." When she gave my son his souvenirs, it was with tears in her eyes. Daddy had bought his grandson a small statue of a penguin. The same penguin he had bought for himself. My son unwrapped Dad's—he died before he could do it himself—and placed it on Dad's desk with souvenirs from other trips. They also brought my son two T-shirts— one from the Falkland Islands and one from Ushuaia, the end of the world. Dad always enjoyed giving my son presents after a trip. His eyes always sparkled with excitement. Now, they will never sparkle again.

I associate Billy Joel with travel, because of Dad, because Dad loved his music and always listened to him in the car. When I was a child and we went on family vacations, Billy Joel was always the first person we listened to early in the morning when we got on the road. I still hear "Movin' Out" in my memories when I drive over the Verrazano Bridge. A few years ago, I told my son how much Dad liked Billy Joel. My son got it into his head that every time we drove to New York to see his grandparents, we had to listen to Billy's Greatest Hits. We'd get up at five o'clock in the morning to drive out to Long Island, and as soon as I turned the key in the ignition, I'd play Billy. We'd drive in the opposite direction from my memories over the Verrazano listening to music, the past and present colliding in my mind. Last year for Christmas, my parents bought my son a CD player and his very first CD—Billy Joel's *Greatest Hits*. Today, when my son and I got home, the first thing he did was put on Billy Joel's music. As I ironed his shirts—he wore lots of button-down shirts in my absence—and he started on an Abraham Lincoln puzzle, we listened to Billy, my mind flooding with images of Dad and all the times he would sing along in the car.

After dinner, my son dyed eggs. It was sad. We had promised him that Easter was only delayed, not canceled, but the hope was Dad would come home. When he came home, we'd have a happy Easter reunion. Obviously, that's not going to happen, but I still have to keep my promise. It was hard for me to watch my son color eggs. It's something he has always done with Mom out on Long Island. But I guess this marks the beginning of a new era. Slowly, we will all have to learn to let go of what we were used to, what we loved, what we had come to expect.

Snapshot Rewind
Sometime in the 1980s: Daddy didn't like vegetables. He was, according to Mom, "a true German" when it came to his diet—meat and potatoes—but he did eat a few things that were green. One day—it was probably a holiday, but I don't remember which one—

we were visiting my aunt and uncle in Edison, New Jersey, and my grandfather was there. Dad decided to try asparagus and discovered it wasn't so bad. In celebration of Dad trying something new—a rarity—my grandfather rang the bell my aunt had hanging in her kitchen. Dad was mortified. But every time I eat asparagus, I remember the bell and Dad and my grandfather's excitement.

DAY 35

APRIL 19, 2020

I woke up early, but couldn't force myself out of bed. At around seven o'clock, my son crept into my room and wiggled his way into my arms. I held him, and he fell back to sleep. Holding him brings comfort, but it doesn't erase the pain or take away the emptiness.

As promised, the Easter Bunny came and hid eggs. He also left a chocolate bunny and the Bon Jovi CD my son wanted. We didn't want him to feel as if he had been forgotten, as if Easter never happened, but in retrospect, ignoring it might have been the better option. Usually, when he gets stumped in his egg search, he wants a hint. So, I offered him one. "Did you check the fireplace?" This set off another firestorm of angry words and scathing accusations, "Why are you telling me? I don't want help. I don't even want this Easter. I wanted a different Easter." He shouted at me, then added, as he ran into his room and slammed the door, "This isn't any fun. Not like you would know."

Oh, I know. I know exactly how he feels. This isn't the Easter I wanted either. I wanted the same one he did. One in which we were out in Mattituck—with Grandpa. I know precisely how terrible it is to try and recapture the essence of something when the man who always made it perfect is gone. I tried. I wanted to give my son something. But I completely understand his pain, so I let him vent and I cried, my spouse pulling me into her arms so that my tears soaked the shoulder of her robe.

Bonnie is probably correct. My son is taking his pain out on me because he's close to me and I'm a safe target. I also think another friend, Dale, was correct when he said my son is beginning to realize that I don't control as much as he always thought. This awful disease is beyond my control, and despite my best efforts, I couldn't protect or save his grandfather. And as Dale pointed out, "He's lost his male ally in the family, his main male role model." Without him around, everything is going to be harder, at least initially.

It's not just the disease that I can't control. I also can't control the way people react to it and the restrictions implemented because of it. As a result, I've started to unfriend people on Facebook. The callous remarks they make about people dying are painful to read. And the overt praise of Trump, a man I hold responsible for my dad's death—because of his incompetent response to the pandemic—is too much. I am growing increasingly angry at people who are accusing Murphy and Cuomo of being too much like dictators, when they are trying desperately to save lives. I hate being trapped inside. But I understand the necessity perhaps too well. Yeah, losing a job sucks—I know, I lost mine—but having a parent die is far worse. I completely understand that people are frustrated that they can't go hiking or out to eat, but Dad will never do anything again—ever. If stricter measures were in place sooner, then perhaps he'd still be with me. I simply can't waste my time with people whose core moral beliefs and core ethics are incompatible with mine.

In my absence from New Jersey, my coffee mug chipped. It's yellow and it has a picture of the old school library slips on it. I've drank my morning coffee out of it for years, but when I noticed the chip, I threw it away. This upset my son, so he rescued it from the trash, took out his paints, and painted the chip in an attempt to fix it for me. This, less than half an hour after he stormed into his room. It's reassuring to know that he is still sweet and considerate when his pain isn't ripping him apart.

After dinner, my son and I returned to New York to be with my mother. The weekend was rough for her. The drive into Queens was sad. New York used to be my happy place. The place I went to escape my unhappiness in New Jersey. But without Dad, the house feels empty. My son and I were in the car for about ten minutes when he asked, "Aren't you going to play Billy Joel?" I was surprised. While we always used to listen to Billy, things are different now.

"Are you sure you want to listen to him?" I asked.

"Of course. It's what we always do." And so I put Billy on and cried for most of the drive because nothing will ever be as it once was.

When we got to Mom's (my son is still referring to the house as Nonna and Grandpa's), I felt Dad's absence immediately. Always, Dad had been the one to meet us at the back door because Mom's knees are bad, and walking down the stairs is harder for her. But of course, he wasn't there to spread his arms wide and exclaim, "Hey pal, how ya' doin'?" when my son stepped out of the car. As I walked in, I paused to give Mom a hug, and brushed away my tears.

Mom is now cuddling with my son on Dad's chair, and they are laughing together while watching *Peter Rabbit*. Maybe they will ultimately be able to help each other begin to heal.

Snapshot Rewind
Winter 2011: Daddy kept the sled. It was an heirloom that had belonged first to his older siblings, then to him. All my cousins used it. And when my brother and I outgrew it, Dad put it in his

garage where it sat for years waiting for the birth of his grandchild. When my son turned a year old, excitement radiated out of Dad as he pulled it out of the garage and gave it to me. The sled was perfect for a toddler because it had a back to hold him up. During a snowstorm in February, we—Mom, Dad, my son, and I—went up to Juniper Valley Park. Dad enjoyed pulling my son in the sled. And my son smiled, warmly wrapped in a blanket, while Dad took him on a snowy tour of the park. The two of them always seemed to complete each other.

DAY 36

APRIL 20, 2020

Daddy insisted on taking $200 dollars to the hospital. Mom doesn't understand why, and it has troubled her since the day I drove Dad to Columbia Presbyterian. My guess is Daddy expected to come home. He, like me, thought he was going into the hospital to get better, not to die. And when he came home, he didn't want to trouble me again. He wanted to have money for a cab. Of course, nothing would have made me happier than driving back into Manhattan to bring him home. It's what I wanted, and I would have done it gladly—even with traffic. But numerous times, Mom has told me that he didn't want to worry me. He didn't want to trouble me, which is why my mother didn't call until four-thirty when she should have called hours earlier. I will always regret not giving Dad one final hug. But I can at least find some solace in knowing that when Daddy needed me, I was there immediately. So to all the older children out there, be kind to your parents. Visit them often, and if they ask you for something, do it quickly and without complaint because it might be the last thing you ever get to do for them. And to all the elderly parents out there, if your children are half as close to you as I was to my dad, they are already worrying about you—and the worry will stretch beyond this pandemic. If you are not feeling well, or something doesn't feel right, call your children. They love you. They want to be there for you.

Every morning, I walk around the cemetery, which is teeming with gravediggers, and I cry. Every day they are digging new graves because people are dying at a rate unseen since the Spanish Flu pandemic a century ago. Today—by eight a.m.—there were six new graves and a seventh being dug. Seven mounds of earth piled high to make room for seven new coffins. Seven other families who are now in pain and grieving as we are. It's too many. It didn't have to be like this. A responsible federal government would have made efforts to control it sooner.

While I walk, I usually read, but lately, I am having a great deal of difficulty reading. Reading has always been somewhat of a struggle for me. I know, I read incessantly, and I enjoy it, but that doesn't mean it's something that comes easy to me. I read slowly. I always have, which is one reason I detest timed tests. Dad always poked fun at how slowly I read. He read slowly, too, but not as slowly as me. If I try to speed up, the words get jumbled up in my head, jammed like the keys of an old-school typewriter. Also, my short-term memory isn't the best, which means to truly grasp what I'm reading, I often read sentences, paragraphs, or even entire pages more than once. If the paragraph is long, I sometimes forget what I read in the beginning by the time I get to the end. But I also have difficulty sitting still, which is why I do the majority of my reading while in motion. When I'm moving, my brain tends to process things more efficiently. But lately, reading, even while in motion, is hard. I can't concentrate at all. I read a few sentences and my mind is exhausted. Comprehension hurts my head.

Before Dad got sick, I ordered *Pale Rider: The Spanish Flu of 1918 and How It Changed the World*. I enjoy history because it often offers a road map for the present. Besides, while I consider myself knowledgeable about history, I knew virtually nothing about the Spanish Flu. As always, when made aware of holes in my historical knowledge, I try to fill them. As I peer through the lens of our recent pandemic, the book is fascinating. People, apparently, have a propensity for being enraged at governments that attempt to institute strict laws in an effort to protect citizens from an epidemic.

Also, people tend to be suspicious of science, fearing conspiracy theories instead of trusting that maybe scientists—when it comes to disease—do know best. So much of what I'm reading can be applied to today.

I am not the only one struggling to read. Yesterday, my son finally read the last page of *Hound of the Baskervilles.* One page, that was all. He refused to start a new book.

For school, on the morning "Welcome Wall," my son was supposed to write about something for which he is grateful. He read the assignment, looked at me, his lower lip trembling, and said, "How can I be grateful for anything? I don't have Grandpa anymore." While I can think of many things he is grateful for—or should be grateful for—right now he can't see beyond his pain, his loss. Seriously, Grandpa was his everything. So I told him to skip the assignment.

Between trying to help my son with schoolwork, while he worked in his bedroom, and supporting Mom, while she made phone calls in the kitchen to sort out Dad's affairs, I spent much of the morning running up and down the stairs. I got a complete workout toggling between the two of them. Except for one burst of frustration over math, my son has been cooperative. The really hard call Mom had to make was to Viking Cruises to get her money back. Dad had booked a 50th anniversary cruise for them in the fall of 2021. They were supposed to visit several ports in Europe. Mom cried the whole time she was on the phone with a representative. All I could do was put my arm around her and hold her while she tried to get the words out. A second call was to Tripmate, an intermediary company used by Viking Cruises. Mom and Dad cut their trip in South America short because Argentina closed her borders due to the pandemic. They were supposed to go to Iguazu Falls, but they never got there. Mom had to call for her refund. While on that call, the agent asked for my dad's name and Mom started to cry again. She explained why she was so upset through her tears, "I'm sorry. My husband just died from COVID," but the sobs swallowed her words. I had to take the phone from her. It was too emotional of an experience for Mom. The agent was so upset to hear the news that she, too, started crying.

Before Mom and Dad went on vacation, Mom had been having a recurring dream. She needed to get home, but she didn't know why. In the dream, she thinks she was somewhere in New Jersey, but she wasn't entirely certain. Since she didn't know how to get home, she started to walk. Her travels took her through a rundown neighborhood. At some point, she saw a ferry in the distance and headed toward it. As she was approaching it, she saw a lighthouse, but she had to be careful walking because the water was rough. It crashed against the shore, and she was afraid she'd get hurt on the rocks. But she made it to Hoboken, which is where she spent her childhood, after her parents immigrated from Sorrento. But it wasn't the Hoboken she remembered. The dream skips ahead to a train ride, followed by a bus ride which drops her where she lives now. But when she got there, she knew something was wrong. She didn't live on that block anymore. And that's when she woke up— each time—feeling extremely unsettled.

Last weekend was belt promotions and graduation for Taekwondo—via Zoom. I didn't go. Everything was still too raw. My instructor told me to take as much time as I needed and that he'd let me graduate when I felt ready. I wasn't ready tonight—not really—but I did it because I know Daddy would have been disappointed if I didn't. When it came to sports, he was always my number-one fan. I couldn't have had a more supportive parent. Back in November, I decided it was time to resume studying Taekwondo.

I looked forward to getting my black belt someday, and assumed Dad would be there to watch me test. I wanted him to hug me, congratulate me, and tell me he was proud of me. Then maybe we would have all gone out for dinner to celebrate. He had been there for every other sports achievement in my life. But he won't be there anymore. This evening, I was promoted to brown belt. It's a minor achievement, but it's the first I've had without Dad. Had he been alive, he'd have been the first person I called.

Snapshot Rewind
Summer 1995: I was dating a guy—yes, a guy, my long painful coming out was still a couple of years in the future and the subject of another memoir—from Southold, Long Island. He loved to play golf, but he also enjoyed a competitive game of miniature golf, which was the extent of my golfing skills. One evening, Dad suggested a double date—Mom, Dad, me, and my boyfriend. Dad took us all out to play mini-golf in Calverton. It was fun. Of course, Dad won, beating my boyfriend by one stroke. Dad always won. No matter how well I played, he played better. After the game, Dad took us all out to Friendly's for ice cream.

DAY 37

APRIL 21, 2020

My son has turned into Jekyll and Hyde. By day, he's a storm to be reckoned with, raging against me and anything else that gets in his way. The slightest things set him off. His anger is explosive. By night, he is a cuddle-bug, desiring nothing more than the comfort of my arms. He comes into my room and wants me to hold him. Periodically, he wakes and adjusts his body, wrapping his arm more securely around me or snuggling closer so that I can hold him more tightly. He is experiencing two faces of grief simultaneously.

Daddy died a week ago. I still can't wrap my head around how quickly the virus came and stole him from us. But it didn't come from nowhere. Generally, I pride myself on being up to date with news (though lately it's too painful to watch or read), but obviously, I wasn't paying close enough attention earlier this year. I should have realized once the virus arrived, once it had spread beyond China, that we would be in danger. I should have been aware that traveling was not wise. I should have begged my parents not to go away. To cancel their trip. But I didn't. I didn't track the virus closely enough. I didn't arm myself with the information that could have saved my dad. But even if I had followed things more closely, I know Dad. He wouldn't have listened. He would have argued that he'd be fine. Because he loved those cruises and wouldn't have wanted to miss it. He wouldn't have believed that it could end so tragically.

When I take a step back, I know there really isn't anything I could have done. But when I look over the last two months, my anger at

Trump multiplies. His stupidity, his ego, his selfishness have killed many Americans. In an attempt to make sense of my dad's death—in conjunction with Trump's lies—I've constructed my own timeline.

January 22, 2020
The first U.S. case of COVID-19 is reported in Washington State.

Trump declares, "We have it totally under control. It's one person coming in from China." Needless to say, he lied. Almost everything he says is a lie. A week later, there are five cases in the United States. It is definitely not under control.

February 24, 2020
Trump announces, "The coronavirus is very much under control in the USA ... stock market beginning to look very good to me." I remember when he said that. I remember my anger surging over the fact that he was more concerned about money than the virus. I should have realized then that things were extremely ominous. That he was hiding the truth in order to protect the economy. Maybe I did. I don't remember.

February 26, 2020
There are fifty-nine cases in America.

My parents fly down to Chile.

Looking back—and keep in mind, Trump had far more intel than I did; he was well aware of how bad the virus was and how quickly it could spread, or he should have been—I honestly believe Trump should have shut the borders and prevented anyone from traveling well before my parents left. At the very least, he should have issued a severe travel warning. He could have kept them—and others—

safe. But his comment two days earlier indicates that he didn't care about my parents. He didn't care about the health and safety of any Americans. He focused only on making money. He didn't want the economy to crash. Shutting the borders might have done just that. On the day my parents left, Trump knew the cases were rising, but instead of using the information to prevent further spread, he said, "The fifteen cases within a couple of days is going to be down close to zero." Again, he lied. Bastard. We are so far from zero.

February 27, 2020
The day after my parents leave, Trump makes his most ridiculous claim. "One day it's like a miracle, it will disappear." Did anyone believe him? I scoffed at his comment. I wanted to throw something at the television. But I didn't yet have a clue that his callous attitude would hurt me and my family so deeply. (Exactly one month later, I would take my dad to the hospital where he would die. There were no miracles, not in the disappearance of the disease, nor in regard to my father.)

February 28, 2020
Trump claims "[COVID-19] is [the Democrats] new hoax." A hoax! Seriously? This phrase will be embraced by his supporters to downplay the virus and demean families like mine who lost a loved one.

My father, in Chile, writes a postcard to my son in which he states, "Looking forward to a great time." If only he knew what awaited him, but how could he when the president back home called it hoax.

March 4, 2020
There are 153 cases.

I have a department meeting at work. We are told that we need to plan how we will teach remotely in case the university moves to online teaching due to the pandemic. One of my colleagues jokes, "I was hoping for one more snow day, not a pandemic." We all laugh. None of us knew what was coming. I ask, "How serious is this? Does the university actually plan on stopping in-person classes, or is this just to appease the powers that be?" My boss shrugs. She isn't sure. At the time, it seemed so freaking extreme.

March 10, 2020
COVID-19 cases in New York start to spin out of control. There are over 600 cases in the United States. But Trump claims, "We are prepared, and we're doing a great job with it. And it will go away. Just stay calm. It will go away." If he was doing a great job, why are there suddenly so many cases? Lies, so many lies.

And I am anything but calm. I am deathly afraid for my parents who are still in Patagonia. Suddenly, this virus is all too real. And I just want my parents home. I want to be able to protect them. I message my dad and my cousins in regard to my son's Taekwondo tournament and our family reunion. "I was really looking forward to seeing everyone at G3's tournament in New Hampshire. But in light of the coronavirus, I do not think it wise for any of you to go to the tournament. It will be a crowded venue with far too much chance of germs spreading, and I want everyone to remain healthy. There will be other tournaments. I would suggest you guys skip the tournament and we meet for dinner afterward, but there is a chance that we would be exposed to something during the tournament. And I wouldn't want to pass it along. I'm hoping things are under control by the end of the month, and if they are we can reconsider. G3 is extremely sad. He was looking forward to seeing everyone as much as he was looking forward to competing. But as of now, the numbers are going up, not down." I went on to comment to my cousins, "I'm worried about Mom and Dad who are on a cruise and will eventually need to fly home."

My cousin responds, "They're on a cruise NOW?!?!? Where?"

I explain, South America "and I'm home hoping they get back safely. However, NYC, I suppose, isn't exactly safe either at the moment."

My dad joins in the conversation to say, "When I got home, I was going to tell you that we won't come to the tournament. I am sad but at our age if we get the virus we could die. I'm thinking of moving to Mattituck for the duration. P.S. no one is sick on our boat." He is trying to alleviate my concern. But by now, I am tracking the virus closely, and I am scared.

Later that day, I get an email from my boss. Beginning the following week, all classes are moving online. The pandemic is no longer a distant fear. In less than a week after our meeting, the wave is crashing upon us.

March 12, 2020
My son comes home from school with a computer. Fear erupts inside of me. The signal is loud and clear; schools are closing their doors, and it would only happen for a good reason. My thoughts are confirmed later that evening by an email from his principal, stating that classes would continue remotely, at least until after Easter.

The NBA suspends play for the season.

Disney closes its parks.

Crap! How did we go from, "The fifteen cases within a couple of days is going to be down close to zero" to the world is shutting down—in two weeks?

March 13, 2020
My cousin messages me, "Any concerns about your parents getting home?"

I am now in panic mode. My parents are all I can think about, but Dad keeps telling me they are fine. "If they have concerns, they haven't shared them. I'm worried. I've been following the outbreak in Argentina, and it is escalating there, too. They also have a travel ban in place, but I don't know the specifics."

March 15, 2020
Cases skyrocket to 3,499.

Trump continues to lie and mislead the American public. He states, "This is a very contagious virus. It's incredible. But it's something that we have tremendous control over." Do we? Really? What evidence is he drawing from? What are the facts that lead him to believe he or anyone else has any control over this?

March 16, 2020
There are more than 1,000 new cases.

My parents return from Argentina. I breathe a sigh of relief that they are here. But I know there is up to a two-week incubation period. If I don't keep busy, fear will fester.

I start my blog as a lark. It was never supposed to be serious.

March 17, 2020
Mom has what she thinks is a head cold that she caught on the plane because it was chilly. But I hear her cough. I suspect it is something more.

March 22, 2020
Dad feels nauseous. He has no appetite and doesn't eat dinner.

March 23, 2020
There are now 43,667 Americans who have tested positive, most of whom are in New York.

Dad starts coughing and he spikes a fever. He calls to get tested for COVID-19, and whomever he speaks to promises that they'll call back within four days to set up a time.

But Trump doesn't care about my father, or anyone else, who is sick. It's obvious that money means more to him than human life, especially when he says, "America will again, and soon, be open for business—very soon—a lot sooner than three or four months that somebody was suggesting ... We cannot let the cure be worse than the problem." I don't give a shit about the economy or things opening up. I'm too busy racing to New York with Tylenol for Dad because I want him to get better, and I'm willing to do anything as long as he doesn't succumb to the virus.

March 26, 2020
In three days, the numbers nearly double. There are 83,836 infected Americans.

I don't like the way Dad sounds. I suspect he isn't breathing well. He tells me not to worry. That he will be okay. That he doesn't need to go to the hospital. I have the first of many emotional break-downs because I feel so helpless.

Trump continues to piss me off. He says, "I don't believe you need 40,000 or 30,000 ventilators. You know, you go into major hospitals sometimes they'll have two ventilators, and now all of a sudden they're saying, 'Can we order 30,000 ventilators?'" Why does he refuse to listen to intelligent people? Scientists and doctors? Experts who know what's really going on in the world?

March 27, 2020
Confirmed cases reach 101,657, one of whom is my father.

Mom calls me at four thirty-three a.m. I take Dad to the hospital, and I never see him again.

Here's the thing: Trump either knew how bad things were going to get and he just didn't care, or he refused to listen to the people who had a clue, thereby remaining ignorant. I'm reading *Pale Rider*—a book about the Spanish Flu pandemic—by Laura Spinney. On page 91, what she says in regard to the flu in 1918 can easily be applied to today:

"In these modern cites, anti-infection measures had to be imposed from the top down, by a central authority. To pull this off, the authority required three things: the ability to identify cases in a timely fashion, and so determine the infections direction of travel; an understanding of how the disease spread (by water? air? insect vector?) and hence the measures that were likely to block it; and some means of ensuring compliance with those measures."

Let's break it down. Trump is the president. It was his job to hire the right people to immediately identify cases of COVID-19. In

2018, Trump disbanded the pandemic response team. He didn't care enough, and therefore, he was left unprepared. Still, he knew it was here, and instead of instituting strict regulations, instead of going on the offensive, he played the "we have it under control card." When that didn't work, he called it a hoax. He chose to lie. To me. To my parents. To you.

Trump should have known how it was spread. Instead of attacking China, he should have been collecting information. Finding out everything they knew about it in an effort to prevent it from spreading here. He could have minimized the outbreak if he had shut the borders, shut down the economy back in early February, and issued a nationwide stay-at-home order. Yes, it is easy for me to say this now; I have the hindsight. But Trump should have been aggressively seeking information instead of pretending there wasn't a problem. If he had been, he'd have had the necessary information months ago.

Trump is the president. He doesn't shy away from executive orders. If he wanted to, he could have found a way to ensure that citizens complied to strict measures. But he didn't. Why?

Well, according to Spinney on page 99, "But mandating a central authority to act in the interests of the collective potentially creates … problems. First, the collective may have competing priorities—the need to make money, say, or the need to raise an army—and deny or water down the authority's piers of enforcement." And there you have it. Money. Except it wasn't necessarily the collective that wanted to make money, it was the wealthy. And the collective didn't have to water down the central authority because Trump belongs to the wealthy class. His interests were in making money and keeping the economy strong. Not protecting Americans.

Okay … enough babbling. But I needed to get that out. And my brain felt a little less foggy this afternoon.

Today was another rough day for Mom. We had to call Jet Blue to cancel our flight to Florida. Dad had promised my son we'd go to Disney World and Universal Studios this summer. We were supposed to fly down on June 30th. Between the pandemic and Dad's death, we won't be able to go. My son had been looking forward to this trip for four years. If only Dad was still here and the stay-at-home orders were the only issue. If only we could promise we'd go next year, all of us together, our family whole. But we can't. Our family is broken.

After Jet Blue, Mom had to call Social Security. She started to say that Dad died, and again, the sobs overcame her. Having to continuously repeat the words, "My husband died from COVID," is too much for a grieving widow. So, I took the phone from my mother and completed the call for her. When I hung up, Mom was shaking. I hugged her and she said, "I don't know what I'd do if you weren't here. I could never do this by myself."

The day was going well for my son until he got to the part of his schoolwork where he had to read three chapters in *Bridge to Terabithia* and answer questions. He started stomping his feet and slamming doors and shouting that it wasn't fair. He didn't want to do it. He wouldn't do it and I couldn't make him. Quietly, I told him to go upstairs and read. All he had to do today was read. He could answer the questions tomorrow and Thursday. He clomped up the stairs, and I let him be. About twenty minutes later, he was quiet and so I went to check on him. I found him sitting on Grandpa's bed—back to me, legs crossed, and shoulders slumped, so that he appeared to be sinking into the mattress—surrounded by a half a dozen Lego superhero sets that he had constructed with Grandpa.

In his hands, he held the Lego pirate ship they completed the weekend Dad took us to Oyster Bay to visit Teddy Roosevelt's house. My son didn't need to read, he needed time to mourn. To be with his grandfather the only way he knew how.

Leaving him alone, I emailed his teacher. And as I started to write, I remembered crying when I read *Bridge to Terabithia*, because if my memory is correct, one of the characters dies. That is not an appropriate book for my son to be reading now. In my email to my son's teacher, I asked if he could please read *The Lion, the Witch, and the Wardrobe* instead, which is what another group is reading. "It has a happy ending," I explained. "And my son needs happy." She very readily agreed to the change. But that's not for today. I love to read, but just yesterday I wrote about how difficult it has become. How can I ask my son to do something that he perceives as a chore when I am struggling to do it for fun? No, there won't be any more independent reading; not until he's ready.

Dad's cell phone rang. Out of curiosity, I answered it. It was a representative—I think she said—from the New York Department of Health calling to schedule the COVID-19 tests for my parents. My parents called four weeks ago—twenty-nine days to be exact. I wanted my parents tested then, but they never called as promised. My parents' health wasn't important enough. I laughed at the woman. "My dad called you a month ago, and you're only calling back now."

She started to stutter. "I'm sorry we've—"

I wasn't in the mood for excuses. "My dad was sick when he called. Now he's dead. Thank you for killing my father," I spat and then ended the call. My son is not the only one who is angry.

Snapshot Rewind

June 2014: For my son's half birthday—we celebrated his half birthday with friends because his birthday falls so close to Christmas—friends of the family gave him an extremely generous gift that included several Lego sets. My son—four years old—opened the Legos, tossed them aside, and pouted, "I hate Legos. They're boring." I was mortified. My friend handed me the gift receipt as I swallowed my embarrassment. But I didn't return them. Once my son opened the box and started to put together an airplane, he thought Legos were the coolest thing ever. And he came to love doing them most with Grandpa. Every time he visited, he'd bring a Lego set and they'd sit together for hours putting it together. Every year around Christmas, Dad would take us into Manhattan to see the tree and St. Pat's. He'd spoil us with lunch. And always, we'd end up in the Lego store where my son would pick out the Lego set he wanted from my parents for his birthday. The Legos are infused with his grandpa's spirit. No wonder he wanted to do nothing else today.

DAY 38

APRIL 22, 2020

My son is back in New Jersey. I wanted him here. But his explosive behavior was not good for my mother. She isn't doing well either, and his slamming doors and screaming unsettled her even more. This morning, I came home from my walk intending to make my son breakfast. But he had already eaten cinnamon toast and strawberries with whipped cream. The moment I opened the door he yelled at me, "Why did you go walking? You should have stayed home to make me breakfast."

"I told you I'd cook when I got back," I put my hand on his shoulder, trying to calm him. Yesterday, he had asked me to wake up earlier so that I'd be back from my walk sooner to cook. In an effort to appease him, I did just that—waking up at five-thirty. But even that wasn't enough.

He jerked away, "We'll it's too late. You shouldn't have left. You should care about me more than you care about yourself." He stomped up to his room, angry that I wasn't at his beck and call to make him pancakes. He could have waited. He chose not to, but somehow that was my fault. In his mind, if I loved him, I'd have been home when he woke up.

Upstairs, he slammed his door twice, and Mom sagged into herself. Numerous times, I asked my son to please be quiet out of respect for his grandmother. "Nonna is hurting too. She is sad just like you are," I explained, but he continued to rage in his room, banging things and shouting about how I'm the worst mother around. I went up to try to talk to him, and he swung the door, trying to hit me, trying to push me out. "Stay away from me," he screamed. His behavior left me in an impossible position. I know he is acting out of grief and anger that his grandfather is dead. And I want to be there for him. But I also need to be here for my mother. However, it became apparent to me today that my son and my mother can't be in the same house. Not now. And so, feeling emotionally beat up, I drove him back home.

I felt terrible about doing it. But my mother needs peace. My son needs space to vent. I feel torn between the two of them. I'm hoping that my brother will be able to come and be with Mom soon so that my son and I will be able to spend some much-needed time together. Just the two of us. Because along with being angry about his grandfather's death, I think he's mad at me for having been gone for so long. And that's why he told me that he thinks I care about myself more than him. Maybe being away from his grandfather's house, a place in which he is surrounded by memories, will be good for him.

As I drove over the bridge, my guilt multiplied. I feel like a terrible mother. But I'm struggling to be the daughter my mother needs while simultaneously being the mother my son deserves. It hasn't been easy. And I'm vulnerable, too. There are moments when I'm cracking beneath the weight of my own sorrow. How can I hold someone else up when I'm buckling at the knees just trying to keep myself upright? Anyway, as I headed west, I realized my son's breakdown about breakfast probably had very little to do with me and everything to do with Dad. Dad was the pancake king. It wasn't me my son wanted home to make breakfast. It was his grandfather. But he yelled at me because I'm the one still here.

157

While driving, I got a message from Brian, the high school friend who brought me ginger. His father is sick, and they are concerned it might be the virus. I broke down and cried because I know my friend is close to his dad, too. I hate the thought of anyone being in as much pain as I am in right now. How many more children will lose a parent to this awful disease? How many more deaths will leave holes in other people's hearts?

When I returned to Queens, there was more business to tend to for Mom. I had to call Disney to cancel our upcoming vacation. Back in my former life, before the world turned upside down, for several mornings, over FaceTime, we—Mom, Dad, my son, and I—discussed what we were going to do. Which parks we were going to hit, which restaurants we were going to eat in. And now, I was canceling Dad's dream because he died before it could be fulfilled. I'm not sure what saddens me more: the fact that my son won't get to go with his grandfather or the fact that Dad died before he could have one last spectacular time with his grandson. I had to wait for twenty minutes to speak to a representative while listening to "It's a Small World," music that reminded me of Dad and our prior trips to Disney. When someone finally came on the line, I was shaking. I barely got through the call without crumbling. After I hung up, I felt like I'd been hit by a train. Between taking my son home and canceling the vacation he had been looking forward to, I was emotionally spent.

You all know how I feel about Trump. I'm not sure I have ever detested anyone more. Well, I learned, on page 61 in *Pale Rider*, that in an effort to avoid stigmatizing a particular segment of the world's population, "In 2015 the World Health Organization issued guidelines stipulating that disease names should not make reference to specific places, people, animals or food." Therefore, when Trump defiantly referred to COVID-19 as the Chinese virus, he was flouting these guidelines. In essence, he was giving the finger to the World Health Organization and their attempt to prevent open hostility toward people from a certain nation. Is anyone surprised? The man is a vile human being.

Snapshot Rewind

1970: Daddy didn't want to go to Vietnam. He didn't want to die in a war that we never should have been involved with in the first place. He put off the draft as long as he could by extending his time in college by a semester. But he eventually had to graduate. Initially, he passed his physical for the army. But his father called in a favor—I'm sorry, I don't know the details—and requested that Dad have a second physical. One that Dad intended to fail.

While he was in college, Dad and a couple of friends went to Maine for vacation. They went swimming—if I recall properly—at Moose Lake, and Dad developed a sinus infection. At the time, a doctor told him that he would never have problems swimming in salt water, but fresh water could trigger another infection. Knowing this, the day before his second physical, he and Mom went to visit Mom's sister and her husband in New Jersey. While there, they paid a visit to the pool at the country club my uncle belong to. Dad spent the entire afternoon jumping into the water, intentionally trying to destroy his sinuses. It worked.

The following morning, he woke up with an intense headache. As part of Dad's physical, the doctor took an x-ray of Dad's sinuses. All the doctor saw was a cloud. Dad had done exactly what he set out to do. When the nurse—"a big Black man," as Dad described him—came into the room to tell Dad that he failed the exam, Dad jumped up and gave him a hug.

DAY 39

APRIL 23, 2020

As I've already told you, Dad loved his family more than anything. Everything he did, he did for Mom, me, my brother, and my son—especially my son. But as he got older, what he really wanted was some connection to his extended family. Not having that, he felt somewhat unmoored. Several years ago, he saw on Facebook that his sister had met up with a cousin, and he was sad that he hadn't been invited to join them. That's why, last December, when I met Dad's cousin and her daughter at my son's Taekwondo tournament, I made a point of letting them know when we would next be in Massachusetts. They marked the date on their calendars. We all did—even Dad. Over the years, Dad had given me so much, that's why I really wanted to give him this, the connection he so desperately craved. But that dream—like so many others—turned to ashes the day he died.

However, back in mid-January, my son, for a Cub Scout project, needed to interview an older relative to learn how life has changed over the years. I thought he'd want to interview his grandfather, so I was surprised when he insisted on interviewing Anna, Dad's cousin instead. She happily agreed to a FaceTime interview, and we arranged it for when we'd be visiting Dad so that he could say hello. He was so excited the morning of the call. He only spoke with his cousin for a few minutes, but it made him incredibly happy. My son gave that gift—a conversation with a cousin whom my dad hadn't seen in nearly sixty years—to his grandfather. And I am grateful that he did.

That January weekend—the one where Dad and his cousin spoke—was the last time my son saw his grandfather. The last time I saw Dad before he got sick. And it was the last time we went to the movies with him. He took us to see, *Jumanji: The Next Level,* and we all enjoyed it. When we left on Sunday night, my son wanted to linger as he always did, but it was getting late, and he had school the next day. As Dad waved to us, making silly faces at my son the way he always did, my son slumped in the back seat and said, "I already miss Nonna and Grandpa."

I smiled at him in the rearview mirror and responded, "I know you do. But we'll see them again. I promise." But he never did. The virus had not yet arrived in America—or so we believed at the time. How was I to know that I should have let my son stay longer? That I should have turned around and let him stay another day? Another week? If only I had known that Dad would die before we had a chance to hug each other one more time, we would not have left.

My son is back. He wanted another chance, and Mom and I didn't want him to feel unloved or unwanted. My spouse drove him back to New York after the two of them completed their schoolwork for the day. They came in time for dinner. While we ate, I heard from Brian. He took his father to the hospital last night. He tested positive for COVID-19 and is currently on oxygen, but not a ventilator.

Snapshot Rewind
2005: My Dad and I had been close to his family—his brother's branch—out on Long Island. We went to most of my cousins' weddings, countless birthday parties for my cousins' kids, and we spent numerous holidays together. I had even gone on vacation up to Plattsburgh during winter break with my one cousin and her family when I was in college. But fifteen years ago, that all changed.

My spouse and I got married in Canada, but the following month, we had a wedding reception for friends and family. Initially, my dad's family out in Long Island said they'd come, but then the invitations went out and they all declined, stating the fact that New Jersey was too far away. They couldn't make it. They claimed it was the distance. Dad suspected it was because I was marrying a woman. To them, it wasn't a "real" wedding. Dad was angry and hurt—crushed. After all the family functions he'd been to, no one bothered to show up for me. In a silent rage, he announced, "They're all dead to me." And he never spoke to them again.

Four years later, another cousin—Dad's sister's son—got married. Coincidentally, he and his wife had their wedding at the exact location I had my reception. When I pulled up with my parents, we saw our Long Island family milling around outside by the front door. Dad marched right up to them and said, "I guess New Jersey isn't so far after all." And then he walked inside where he proceeded to socialize with the bride's family instead of his own.

DAY 40

APRIL 24, 2020

Today is the fortieth day of my blog. Forty days since the world stopped. Biblically speaking, forty is significant. It represents a period of being tested, a trial. Moses and his people spent forty years wandering through the desert. Noah endured forty days and forty nights of rain on his ark. Jesus fasted for forty days in the wilderness while the devil tempted him. Even Lent, a period of fasting and repenting for Christians between Ash Wednesday and Easter Sunday, lasts forty days. But in Biblical scenarios, forty marks an end, and where I'm sitting right now, I see no end. No end to the deaths, especially in New York. No end to my grieving, my pain. No end to this online remote learning which my son and I detest. These have without a doubt been the worst forty days of my life. If I am being tested, I feel like I am failing. And a test that includes the death of my father is incredibly cruel.

According to ABC News (because different sources have slightly different numbers), 49,963 Americans have died from COVID-19. If you see this number as a statistic, you are one of the lucky ones. But each of these deaths was a person with a face and a family. They were enjoying their lives. They were happy. What I want to see is a giant mural somewhere, a collage with a picture of every person who died. I want these deaths personalized. Because to me, and hundreds of thousands of other family members, this pandemic isn't about the numbers. It's about the people whom we have loved. The people who were taken from us too soon.

Nearly 50,000 Americans dead, most of whom died in the last forty days. And how does our president respond? Does he say anything helpful? Anything meaningful? Anything compassionate? Of course not. Yesterday, during his press conference, after another American official extolled the virtue of disinfectant for killing the virus on surfaces, our brilliant leader suggested that perhaps people should inject disinfectant into their bodies to kill the disease. I kid you not. When I first saw it, I thought it was a joke, someone poking fun of Trump's stupidity. But I was wrong. Trump's exact words were: "And then I see the disinfectant where it knocks it out in a minute. One minute. And is there a way we can do something like that, by injection inside or almost a cleaning? Because, you see it gets on the lungs, and it does a tremendous number on the lungs. So it'd be interesting to check that. So that you're going to have to use a medical doctor, but it sounds—it sounds interesting to me." Really? Did anyone listening think this was a good idea? What doctor would even entertain such a ludicrous concept? When I told my son what Trump said, he responded, "But if people do that, won't it kill them?" And there you go, ladies and gentlemen. My fourth grader is smarter than our commander-in-chief.

What I really miss is being able to call Dad, to laugh with him about Trump's idiocy. I miss the days when it was comical. It's no longer funny. Dad hated him. He couldn't stand him. And in the end, he killed Dad. No, he didn't shoot him or stab him, but his lies, his inactions, and his lack of empathy certainly did kill him. I can't imagine a worse president during a health crisis.

My son asked me to make waffles for breakfast. I didn't want to; I didn't think I was ready. Dad was the waffle maker. Almost every time we visited, he made waffles. Since I was trying really hard to avoid another breakdown, I gave in. As I was gathering the ingredients, I couldn't remember which mixing bowl Dad used to use.

It's such a small thing. Mom has several mixing bowls and any of them would have worked. But I wanted Dad's, and I couldn't remember which one it was, and I slumped to the floor and cried—because I couldn't ask him. Eventually, I picked the yellow mixing bowl. I think, maybe, that's the one he used, but I'm not sure. Usually, my son eats at least three or four waffles, but after eating only one, he announced, "These aren't as good as Grandpa's," and he walked away. I was frustrated but not mad, especially since he's right. It's the same damn recipe, but Dad's always tasted better.

When I first started dating my spouse, I told her I couldn't eat waffles out in restaurants or at anyone else's house because nobody made them as good as Dad. She accused me of being a daddy's girl. Yeah, I couldn't argue with that. However, when it came to waffles, Dad really did make the best. And the first time my spouse ate them, she agreed. But she makes fun of the recipe all the time. When she cooks, she needs precision, and Dad's waffle recipe is anything but precise. Among the directions are "two *or* three eggs." Also, "a little *less* than three cups of milk." And the bits that boggle my spouse the most, "One *good* teaspoon of baking powder and one *heaping* teaspoon of sugar." Good? Heaping? What does that even mean? When I watched Dad, it was more like one heaping teaspoon of baking powder and two heaping teaspoons of sugar. I imitate him as best as I can, and still my waffles fall short.

I believe Dad's waffle recipe started out as his mother's. When my brother and I were kids, sometimes during Lent—a season when meat was forbidden for Catholics on Fridays—we'd have waffles for dinner. At the time, neither Dad nor I ate fish. Dad hated beans and vegetables and pizza, so we didn't have many meal options. We were supposed to be fasting, giving something up, but instead, we ate breakfast for dinner. And since I always hated meat, I looked forward to those Fridays when waffles were on the menu. So much for sacrifice and giving something up.

After breakfast, Mom and my son worked on a puzzle, while I called Universal Studios to cancel our trip. I explained why I was asking for a refund, and the representative told me that the park's policy is to only speak with the person who booked the reservation. "Really!" I sighed in exasperation. "If the person who booked the trip was currently able to make the call, there'd be no need to cancel. Did you not listen to me when I explained why I was canceling? My dad is dead. Not sure how, exactly, you expect to talk to him." I was so emotionally exhausted, I couldn't even raise my voice, but my tone was enough to get her to connected me to a manager who did refund the money.

A writing friend of mine commented on my last blog post, "I felt nothing when my father died—well, with the exception of confusion as to why I just didn't care. Was I lucky or not? You are in so much pain. I wonder if I am better off. However, I am grieving with you over your dad. Something to contemplate anyway."

Her words reminded me of my favorite Garth Brooks song, "The Dance." I would not have wanted to miss any time with my dad. Not one second. I'm in complete agony. I miss Dad immensely. I want him here with me and my son so badly, but for forty-five years, the time with him was spectacular. I wouldn't want to trade a single moment of it for something that might hurt a little less now.

Snapshot Rewind
1961–65: Daddy loved to read, but he wasn't a fan of literature. There were a few classics he enjoyed—*Tom Sawyer*, *Call of the Wild*, *White Fang*, *Mutiny on the Bounty*, and *Men Against the Sea*—

adventure stories, tales that appeal to young boys. He often told me he thought my son would enjoy the books about Captain Bly, and I hoped that someday we'd get to read them together so that my son and Dad could discuss them. But now that will never happen. I mean, we can still read them, but he can't discuss them with Grandpa.

Dad always joked that he never would have survived high school English if it wasn't for the classic comics. He loved them. They broke down the classics without all the flowery language he hated. Descriptions of any sort—of settings or people—bored him. And the comics were apparently true enough to the main plot points that he could do well on tests. And in high school, Dad was a good student. I've never read a classic comic. Comics and graphic novels never appealed to me. Dad always called me an English snob. Maybe I am. But now, I'm curious. If I could get my hands on a classic comic, I'd read it.

As Dad got older, he enjoyed historical fiction novels as well as books that had lots of action. There were few authors that he and I both enjoyed: James Michener, Edmund Rutherford, and Ken Follett. It is undeniable that a love of reading is a Jaeger trait.

DAY 41

APRIL 25, 2020

In my senior year at St. Francis Prep. High School, I took an elective religion class titled "Living with Loss." It had originally been called "Death and Dying," but that was too morbid, so they changed it. Americans like euphemisms. Allegedly, they make things easier, softer, less painful. Anyway, one night for homework, my teacher, who I really liked, told us to draw a picture of the afterlife. I'm like my son. Even on good days, when I wasn't in the heart of the deepest sorrow I've ever experienced, I hated fluff assignments. And the fact that I can't draw probably contributed to my aversion. But I did as I was told—I always did. The next day, my classmates showed up with pictures of clouds, harps, and angels. Heaven. They all drew some version of the Heaven we had been learning about for years. I drew a dark tunnel. When my teacher confronted me about it and asked why I drew that, I told her, "I've never died. I've no idea what exists on the other side." I still don't.

Maybe that's part of my difficulty. I don't have faith. I'm too much like Thomas, who needed to stick his fingers in Jesus's wounds to trust that it really was him who had risen from the dead. If I can't see it, feel it, touch it, how can it be real? I was raised Catholic, but after living in Asia and traveling through various Asian countries, I found myself drawn to Buddhism. For me, there was something peaceful about the meditation process, the looking inward rather than outward.

Before my son was born, I attended a Tibetan Buddhist temple. Part of me likes the idea of reincarnation. The coming back. The having a second chance. But if you carry no memory of what came before, how do you know when you meet someone you once loved? Of course, right now, as my tears fall onto the keyboard, I want to believe in Heaven—a place where I will be reunited with Dad, where I can hug him again, not soon, but someday. But I've learned, especially in the last month, that wanting something isn't enough to make it a reality. And so, without faith, with one foot in Christianity and another in Buddhism, it's hard to find any sort of comfort from the afterlife. It also makes it hard for me to comfort my son. I've lied enough to him—unintentionally about seeing Dad again—I don't want to lie again, promising him a Heaven, a reunion that may never take place. I'm back to being seventeen years old and staring at a dark tunnel because my experiences have given me nothing more tangible to hold onto.

At night, I don't sleep well. After I wake up—as I always do—to go to the bathroom, I go back to bed where my mind drifts to Dad's final conscious moments. The morning I took him to the hospital. Did Dad know that he would die? Did he suspect it? When they put him on the ventilator, was he scared? He didn't sound afraid, only confident, trusting that he'd get better. I wonder, had his brain been affected by his poor breathing at that point? Was it cloudy from lack of oxygen? Daddy was an incredibly smart man. If his mind was working, he must have known he might be close to the end. And before the drugs knocked him out, what were his final thoughts? Did he regret not telling me he loved me one more time? I hope not because he didn't need to say it. He showed me through his actions for forty-five years that he loved me. Did he think of my son, regretting the fact that he might never see him again? I hate to think of his final moments being sad. But how could they have been anything else? I'd like to believe that he drifted off to sleep envisioning his grandson's arms around him as they watched a movie together or dancing with my mom—Daddy loved to dance. Something happy, something that might have brought him comfort. We couldn't be there, but hopefully we gave him the memories he needed to find a bit of solace before he lost consciousness. I hate that we never had any closure. No goodbye, until it was too late.

I left Mom alone so that I could spend the weekend with my son and spouse. I'll go back on Monday, but I feel horrible for leaving. I'm worried about her. She feels guilty about Dad's death, guilty that she didn't me call sooner. But even the doctor said it wouldn't have mattered. For some people, the virus digs in and refuses to let go. Even if we had gotten Dad to the hospital a day or two sooner, he wouldn't have survived. There's nothing the doctors could have done. But Mom still blames herself. She still won't sleep in her bed, the bed she shared with Dad for nearly fifty years. She can barely stand to be in their bedroom, surrounded by his things, memories of him.

Earlier in the week, my Taekwondo instructor dropped off my new belt—brown with a black stripe. Now it feels official, as if I've actually accomplished something. It made me smile, something that doesn't happen often enough anymore.

My spouse has been great about doing extra chores at home while I've been with my mother. Ever since my son was born, I have washed and folded his clothes. But lately, the task has fallen to my spouse, and she has done it willingly, so I won't complain. However, once you see the clothes she has folded, you can't unsee them. There is a reason she doesn't do my laundry. I'm super pain-in-the-ass-anal-retentive when it comes to needing clothes meticulously folded. I did not go through my son's drawers to refold everything she washed. I'm not that psycho, but the clothes that she left on top of the washer, I couldn't resist.

Today, a memory of a conversation I had with my son five years ago popped up on Facebook. In light of yesterday's musing about Dad's waffles, I thought I'd share:

Before bed, G3 likes me to tell him one story about when I was little. Tonight I started a story that ended in a mini-debate.
Me: When I was little, I loved my grandfather's cooking. He was the best cook.
G3: No, my grandfather is the best cook.
Me: Your grandfather is wonderful and amazing and the best at a lot of things, but my grandfather was definitely the best cook.
G3: No, my grandfather is the best cook.
Me: I'm sorry, but my grandfather was the best cook.
G3: Did he make waffles?
Me: No, but he made so many other incredibly delicious dishes.
G3: I don't care. Grandpa makes waffles. He is the best cook.

Also on Facebook, people have been posting about historical accomplishments that resulted during times of rampant infectious disease, times when people kept themselves isolated. Giovanni Boccaccio wrote *The Decameron* during the Black Death in Italy between 1348-1353. During the plague in England in 1666, Sir Isaac Newton spent his time perfecting ideas relating to calculus. The classic kids' board game, Candy Land, came about in 1948. Eleanor Abbott, a teacher, created it to distract patients suffering from polio. I'm not smart enough to be a mathematician. I currently don't have the mental capacity to write a novel, and I'm not creative enough to come up with a clever game for children. But this has become my plague project: a written memorial for my father.

Snapshot Rewind

2019: Last year, my car started to fall apart. It was fourteen years old, definitely time for a new one, but I couldn't afford a car. I've tried for years to find a full-time teaching position, but I remain underemployed. I've been told it's because I'm too expensive—I have three master's degrees and several years of teaching experience—and too stubborn. I worked hard for those degrees, and I refuse to take them off my resume. We, as a family, barely get by as it is, there's no way we were going to be able to buy something as expensive as a car. So Dad said he'd lease me one. I didn't want him to. At my age, I should be self-sufficient and not have to rely on my father. But then one day, I was driving my son home from school, and my brakes died. We couldn't afford new ones. Dad called me up and said, "Now you have no excuse. You need a car. But think of it this way. I'm not leasing you a car. I'm paying for my grandson's transportation so that he can visit me and so that I can spend time with him." I laughed and cried.

That weekend, my spouse and I went looking for cars. We ran into a few problems regarding leasing. First, we had no idea how many miles I should expect to drive per year. If I managed to get a job, the mileage would go up, if not, we didn't have to plan for too many. More importantly, we were too poor to qualify for a lease. Dad was willing to pay, but he wanted to avoid getting entangled with the process. And personally, I much prefer a manual transmission. I wasn't getting one if I had to lease.

With these issues in mind, I set out to find an inexpensive car, one whose monthly payments would be comparable to a lease. Luckily, we stumbled upon a Hyundai Accent for just under $15,000. I felt guilty asking Dad to buy me a car when his offer was to lease one. But in the end, the car would be mine. If I leased a car, I'd have to give it back after three years. Ownership definitely seemed the better deal, not just for me, but for Dad, considering I could keep what he paid for. When I called him up and proposed the idea, breaking down the math, he didn't hesitate. "Get it," he told me. And I did.

Neither one of us had a clue that the car would not only provide transportation for his grandson for another year of visits, it would also be the reason I was able to answer my mother's call. The reason I was able to drive to New York, pick up Dad, and drive him to the hospital with the hope that he would recover.

DAY 42

APRIL 26, 2020

Maybe Daddy was a Jedi. When Obi-Wan Kenobi and Yoda died, their bodies disappeared. Due to the pandemic, we couldn't have a wake. My mother is upset that she couldn't see Dad's body one more time. My rational brain knows he will be cremated. But since I didn't get to see him, the more fanciful part of my brain keeps envisioning his physical body simply vanishing in his hospital bed, transforming into a spirit, and connecting more closely with the force. Except, when Obi-Wan Kenobi and Yoda died, Luke could still hear them talking to him. I can't hear Daddy. Maybe I'm not trying hard enough. Maybe I'm trying too hard.

I'd like to believe his spirit is somewhere watching over me and my son the way Obi-Wan Kenobi and Yoda continued to guide and look after Luke. I'd like to think even though I can't see him, that he can see me. I want to be able to tell my son that Grandpa isn't gone completely, that he is still smiling down on him and that he will still be able to see all his accomplishments. That he will continue to be proud of the good things he does. But I've already said I have no faith, and I'm too old to believe in fairy tales.

Four years ago, Dad took my son—and Mom and me—to Disney World. We had a wonderful time. When we came home, I made a collage of our trip for my parents and another—with different pictures—for my son. My son's collage was all about the characters he met, but Dad was in some of the pictures, too. In every picture, everyone is smiling. Happy. Last night, my son took the framed collage off his wall and he fell asleep hugging it. His grandfather once filled so many roles—grandfather, father, friend, cheerleader, hero, dream maker—no wonder the hole in my son's heart is so big.

Dad always made the best egg sandwiches. Every time Dad made them, and he made them often for me in the summer when we visited, I commented that they were the best. (If you are sensing a theme here, you are correct. Breakfast was Daddy's favorite meal. The only meal he cooked regularly when we visited.) This morning, as my spouse fried up bacon for breakfast, I couldn't resist remembering. The words were out before I could reign them in. "Dad's egg sandwiches were the best."

My spouse shook her head. "I never really liked them that much."

I sighed. "Well, you're certainly entitled to that blasphemous opinion."

My son, with the help of my spouse, is making a video so that he can complete his reading work for the week. It was due on Friday, but his teacher has been very accommodating, recognizing that school is not terribly important for my son at the moment. I appreciate her kindness. However, it occurred to me this morning that my father wasn't a stranger to her. She met him back in October.

At the beginning of the school year, once a week, the teacher had career day in which parents came into class and discussed their jobs. One afternoon, the teacher emailed me asking if my father would be interested in coming in to talk about what he did for a living. She went on to say that she knew my son and his grandfather were close, so if that was something my dad would like to do, she'd love to have him. Dad was never a kid person. There were only three kids he ever really liked, and the thought of going into a fourth-grade classroom and having to address a group of nine-year-olds unnerved him. But his grandson said please. And he never said no to him. Besides, as I've already stated, Dad always showed up. He was always present.

Dad wrote out notes so that he'd be prepared. According to Mom, "Your father was nervous. For several days, he went over in his mind what he would say and how he would say it. He planned to start out by introducing himself and then asking the kids to introduce themselves so that he could get to know them a bit." Since he was visiting around Halloween, he called me up to ask if he could buy candy for my son's classmates. That's just the type of person he was, wanting to give gifts to everyone. But school rules prohibit parents and others from bringing in food. Too many allergies. I suggested cute Halloween themed pencils instead. Dad was happy to get them.

The day of the presentation, he was invited to have lunch with my son and his teacher. He drove to New Jersey early to pick up Chinese food for himself and my son. He also picked up Duncan Donuts—for him, my son, and my son's teacher. I dropped Dad at school, and when my son came to meet his grandfather in the lobby, he was smiling, excitement pouring out of him. I took a picture of the two of them, knowing it would be one for my annual collage—my son dressed in a black button-down shirt and black pants and Dad wearing a sports jacket and a blue button-down shirt. While Dad was at school, Mom and I went out for lunch.

When I picked Dad up, I could tell by his smile, and the fact that he was very chatty, that he really enjoyed talking with my son's class. What the class enjoyed learning about the most was how computers had changed from Dad's early years as a programmer until now. In Dad's notes, he had written, "You know a computer as something small—handheld—a smartphone or laptop or tablet. When I started work, computers were so big they needed a whole room." A mainframe computer. The concept thoroughly confounded the kids. So that they could see what it looked like, the teacher pulled up pictures on the smart board. I think that afternoon was one of my son's favorite moments in school because he got to show off his grandfather to his friends.

The video did not go well. It turns out my son did not answer the questions for *The Lion, The Witch, and the Wardrobe* sufficiently to be able to record a video. My spouse discovered that when she looked over the directions. Since books are my thing, I offered to help him with his answers before my spouse did the video part. But that was nearly two hours ago. He has been throwing a fit ever since. He claims I'm not willing to help him, but what he wants is for me to tell him what to write. He tells me I don't love him and that I don't care. That I don't understand how upset he is that his grandfather is gone. His anger escalated and he started to shout, "Grandpa always let me do what I wanted. If Grandpa were here, he would care about me. He wouldn't care about school. Grandpa loved me more than you. Grandpa is the one who took me places and did fun things with me. Grandpa wanted to be with me. I want to be with Grandpa, not you."

I know he is grieving. I know he is in pain, but when I try to hug him, he pushes me away. When I try to talk to him, he yells at me. And then, when I back away to give him space, he claims I don't care. And for the record, Grandpa most certainly did care about school. If Grandpa was still here, he wouldn't accept any excuses for not doing work.

After an extremely tumultuous afternoon, we had a calm, quiet evening. We watched the movie *Hound of the Baskervilles*—my son's reward for reading a book. While watching, my son cuddled with me on the couch. I was happy to hold him close without loud or cranky words flying between us, and with his head on my chest, I fell asleep, missing the end of the movie.

Snapshot Rewind
1980–1988: If it were up to me, I'd have been a poor student, but Dad wouldn't stand for it. If I brought home a ninety-eight percent on a test, he'd demand to know what happened to the other two percent. As I got older, he claimed he was joking, but as a kid, the stern look in his eye seemed to tell me that he was most definitely serious.

Every evening, before he came home from work, I had to set my homework out on the dining room table. Before dinner, he would meticulously go through every sentence, every math problem, every answer to make sure it was correct. If it wasn't, he'd get angry. Daddy was never a patient man—not with me, not with anyone, except my son. We had many fights at that dining room table. I shed countless tears. I remember on several occasions screaming that I was stupid and he should just leave me alone. Every single time he answered me by saying, "If you were stupid, I wouldn't expect you to do better. You're smart; that's why I expect you to do well."

Oh, how I hated homework and the wrath of Dad. But now, as a mom, I understand why he did what he did. If he didn't care, he'd have let me slack, he'd have let me hand in crappy work. If he didn't want what was best for me, he wouldn't have driven me so hard to do well.

DAY 43

APRIL 27, 2020

When my son was a toddler, and he was upstairs in his room at my parents' house, or in the bathtub where I had just finished bathing him, he'd call out to Dad. As soon as Dad heard "Bah-Bap," which was how my son pronounced Grandpa when he first started to speak, he'd get out of his chair. His left hand would grab hold of the banister, the wood would creek, and he'd make a trumpeting sound before singing out the words—something about saving the day—from Mighty Mouse. My son, hearing him, would laugh and smile and get excited that Grandpa was on his way.

And it wasn't simply a song lyric. Yesterday, during my son's epic breakdown, I realized how many times Dad actually did save the day, or at least make it less tumultuous. Daddy was often the only one who could calm my son or talk him off an emotional ledge. If my son wouldn't listen to me or my spouse, he'd listen to Dad. If we needed him to do something he refused to do, I appealed to Dad. He had a way of reaching my son in ways no one else could.

When I mentioned this to my spouse last night, she said, "It wasn't just our kid. There were times I had to call your father because he was the only one who could reach you. The only one who could calm you down and get you to see reason. Your father was your lifeline." It's true. He held me together.

As recently as early this winter, not long before my parents left for their cruise, I called Dad one afternoon because my son was being difficult about doing his homework. Dad spoke to him, and then, when my son gave me back the phone, Dad said, "Maybe you need to take it a little easier on him and push him a little less hard in school."

"What?" Was I hearing him properly? Regarding school and my son, I pulled the notes from his playbook. "But you always pushed me!"

"Yes," he agreed, "but I think your son needs to be treated a little more gently." And then he paused, and after a moment, added, "Or maybe I'm softening a bit in my old age. Maybe I was a little too hard on you all those years."

I called Dad for everything. I trusted his opinion, his guidance. But my son and I didn't just call him when we needed something. We spoke to him almost daily, and when something good happened to either of us, he was the first person we'd call. Back in February, when I had my first belt promotion in years for Taekwondo, Dad was the first person I called. Last year, my son came in first place in his Cub Scout pack's pinewood derby. As soon as we got into the car, he wanted to call Grandpa. Two months later, he came in second place for the Bears at the District Championship and qualified for the World Championship at Times Square. Again, the minute we got into the car, he called Grandpa. "And you're going to come to the World Championship, right Grandpa?" he asked, already knowing the answer. Of course, Nonna and Grandpa both came to cheer him on. Dad's last profile picture on Facebook was of him and my son at the Pinewood Derby championship. My son didn't win—not even close. He finished somewhere in the middle of the pack, and then Grandpa took us all out for lunch to celebrate the fact that my son had gotten to compete at Worlds.

What I miss most is hearing his voice. I want nothing more than to be able to call him up. To say hello. To have a conversation with him—about anything.

Several states are planning to partially reopen this week. I'm nothing but a grieving daughter at this point. I'm not a politician or a scientist, but from where I am, it seems irresponsible. I don't have a position that impacts anything. Nothing I say or do can change the course of what we do. But I respect history. Maybe one of the problems with our educational systems is that we teach history incorrectly. Instead of moving through a timeline linearly and discussing events in isolation, we should be teaching students to draw parallels and connections through time. Forget memorizing names and dates and focus on the story, the plot points, the specifics of how learning about the past can prevent similar errors in the present.

This morning, while reading *Pale Rider*, I came across a particularly pertinent passage. On page 205, Spinney recounts:

One 2007 study showed that public health measures such as banning mass gathering and imposing the wearing of masks collectively cut the death toll in some American cities by up to 50 percent (the US was much better at imposing such measure than Europe). The timing of the measures was critical, however. They had to be introduced early and kept in place until after the danger had passed. If they were lifted too soon, the virus was presented with a fresh supply of immunologically native hosts, and the city experienced a second peak of death.

The above discusses the 1918 Spanish Flu pandemic, but it's applicable today. Wearing masks and practicing social distancing are effective measures to cut down infection rates. But if isolation practices aren't in place long enough, more people will die. Keep in mind, we, as a society, are far more mobile than we were a century ago. Sure, we aren't in the midst of a war with soldiers traveling between nations. But we all have cars. And if people in lockdown in one state find that they can travel to another without restraint to get their hair cut or eat in a restaurant or visit a crowded park to take a hike, they will go. Maybe they will carry the virus with them and infect the now-open state. Or they will bring it back to their home state. Either way, it will continue to spread. Why are Americans so selfish? Why is the freedom to get your nails done and to go to a gym more important than someone else's right not to die? I understand being unemployed sucks. Trust me, I've been there. I am there. But you know what sucks even more? When one of the people you love most in the world dies.

And now our brilliant president called the governors encouraging them to open schools. My son is miserable. Our whole family—keep in mind my spouse is a teacher—hates remote learning. A child grieving in a world where he is stuck inside with no outlet is awful. But opening schools seems careless. Yes, we all want to escape our cramped condo. But I'd rather deal with the daily breakdowns my son has than watch as more families suffer the death of a loved one. I don't understand our callousness regarding human life. Why are we so willing to sacrifice people to the god of money? The god of selfishness? The god of inhumanity?

I am back in New York with Mom. She feels like crap. But having me here, she says, eases her loneliness. I guess that's something.

182

Snapshot Rewind

2009–2010: My water snagged a leak the night of December 30. In the morning, I called my parents to let them know their grandchild was on his way. They were heading off to Mohegan Sun, one of the casinos in Connecticut, but Dad asked me if they should cancel their plans and head back to Queens instead. I told him it wasn't necessary. I suspected the baby was in no rush to be born. At least, I hoped he wasn't. I didn't want a December baby. I'd always thought of the week between Christmas and New Year's Day as a dead week.

"Are you sure?" he asked. If I wanted him not to go, he wouldn't have gone.

"I'm sure."

The entire day, Dad worried. (I didn't yet realize that worrying is a manifestation of love. The more you love someone, the more you worry.) My spouse called him periodically to keep him updated, but labor was slow and tedious. So slow that my son wasn't born until 22:32 on January 1—almost forty-eight hours after my water sprung a leak.

While I was in recovery—I ended up having a C-section—my spouse called my parents. Dad answered, and she told him the news, adding, "He looks just like you." They couldn't wait to meet him, and the next morning they enthusiastically drove into New Jersey to spend the first of many happy moments with their grandson.

I always knew my mother wanted a grandchild. That a grandchild would make her happier than anything else. But I didn't know how badly Dad wanted to be a grandfather until my son was born. From the first moment he held him at the hospital, their lives seemed to center around each other.

DAY 44

APRIL 28, 2020

Daddy died two weeks ago. This morning, when I came home from my walk, Mom was crying. She had seen a news segment that indicated that people who are unconscious, and on a ventilator, can hear what people say. When she told me, I felt a little better. It meant Dad heard me when I said goodbye, when I told him I loved him, and it meant that he heard my son's voice, via the video, one final time. But it upset Mom, "I didn't say enough. I should have said more when we said goodbye."

Deaths in America, from the virus, have—as of today—surpassed the number of Americans who died in Vietnam. The Vietnam War lasted a decade. People started dying from the coronavirus three months ago. Well, Trump did promise that he'd do things bigger and better than anyone else. I suppose he fulfilled that promise.

I kept away from the news long enough. Slowly, I'm trying to return to being more informed. Here is what I am learning. According to NBC News, the first confirmed case of COVID-19, in New York City, was on March 1—four days after my parents left for their cruise. However, *The New York Times* reported that there were probably up to 11,000 people infected before then. The first of which may have been as early as late January—an entire month before my parents left. Also disturbing is the fact that the first death—in the United States—seems to have occurred on February 6th, much sooner than originally reported.

A recent *Washington Post* report claims that several U.S. Intelligence Agencies had been warning the president of the severity of the virus as far back as January. Warnings appeared repeatedly in the president's daily brief, but instead of passing on the pertinent information to the Americans, he continued to pretend it was no big deal. I've said before, my parents never should have been allowed to leave the country. I assumed that Trump had the intelligence information to protect my father, and thousands of others, if he desired to do so. Apparently, I was correct. And Trump just didn't care enough to do anything proactive.

In late January, he banned travel from China, but as always, there were exceptions, and some people continued to travel from ground zero to America. Besides, the ban only affected one country. We live in an extremely mobile world. Blocking one border wasn't enough. NBC reported back on April 9, when Dad was still in the hospital, that a study, conducted by Mount Sinai, demonstrated that most cases entered the States from Europe via Kennedy Airport in Queens, New York. Kennedy is eight miles away from where my parents live.

My spouse has argued that perhaps shutting the borders completely in February might have been a bit extreme. If Trump had done that, before people realized the extent of the problem, he'd have gotten quite a bit of pushback. But she, too, faults our president. "If Trump had told the truth from the beginning, if he had gone on television and announced that we were on the verge of a pandemic that could potentially kill hundreds of thousands of Americans, your father would have been able to think about things differently. You're right. He wouldn't have listened to you. But he was a smart man. If he knew the severity of the situation, he could have made an informed decision and stayed home. Trump denied him that." I still would have liked to have seen Trump shut the borders, but I'd have settled for honesty. The biggest problems were the lack of information given to the American people and the lies Trump disseminated instead of facts—reality. My spouse is right. Dad was exceptionally logical. If he knew the facts, the danger he was in—remember, he said he wasn't going to my son's tournament because by then the truth was seeping out—he never would have left. He very well might still be alive.

But Trump continues to be evasive. His emphasis remains not on the people and protecting us but on the economy. Money is all that man talks about. Money and his ego. He wants us to feel indebted to him personally, which is why he insisted on signing all the stimulus checks. His self-praise is nauseating. "I'm sure people will be very happy to get a big fat beautiful check and my name is on it." Really? "A big fat beautiful check?" It's twelve-hundred dollars. All things considered, it's not that much. It doesn't cover my monthly mortgage payment, and I live in a tiny condo. Rent in many places is more. And if people aren't working, how is one relief check really helping? Once you pay your rent, you still have to feed your family.

What I'd like to see, instead, is his name on the death certificate of every American who died from the coronavirus. At the bottom of each certificate it should read, "Donald J. Trump cared more about his ego and the economy than (insert person's name) life." Checks will be cashed, and no one will keep a record of his signature on them. But death certificates are part of the historical record. Historians use them all the time. Therefore, he wouldn't be forgotten. Trump wants to be the biggest and the best. He wants to claim he did things better than any other president. So why not give this to him? Let him take credit for all the deaths. All the lives he ruined. After all, it's what he deserves. I thought Jackson was a bastard for causing the deaths of roughly 6,000 Cherokee on the Trail of Tears. And Johnson was responsible for the deaths of 58,000

Americans because he escalated the war in Vietnam. Trump outdid the both of them—and in a much shorter span of time. Let that be his legacy—American deaths.

Along with a relief check—so measly it won't even cover a year of my son's Taekwondo tuition—Trump sent out a letter to Americans praising himself for a job well done. The letter begins, "Our great country is experiencing an unprecedented public health and economic challenge as a result of the global coronavirus pandemic. Our top priority is your health and safety." Is this where I'm supposed to laugh? How can he even justify saying that? At what point has he demonstrated that anyone's health or safety is important to him? The letter continues, "As we wage total war on this invisible enemy, we are also working around the clock to protect hardworking Americans like you from the consequences of the economic shutdown. We are fully committed to ensuring that you and your family have the support you need to get through this time." What? He doesn't really expect me to believe he is waging total war on the virus. He is encouraging states to open up which will give the virus room to grow and spread. That's the exact opposite of waging war against something. If he wants to make sure Americans have the financial support they need, well, it's going to cost him much more than twelve-hundred dollars per person. If he were as generous as he claims to be, if he dug deep into the treasury and dished out the money people genuinely need—enough for rent, bills, food—then maybe people wouldn't be clamoring to go back to work. If people didn't have to worry about going hungry, they'd be more willing to stay at home in an effort to help prevent the spread of disease.

The final paragraph begins "Every citizen should take tremendous pride in the selflessness, courage and compassion of our people." Excuse me. Yes, there are Americans who are currently being completely selfless. But not Trump. Not the Republicans. I have seen not a single act of courage, compassion, or selflessness from our president or our current presidential administration, especially since the onset of this pandemic. In the wake of Dad's death, I find this letter extremely insulting.

Unlike Trump, Dad was very generous, and not just to his family. Mom always said that organizations would call asking for donations, and Dad almost always reached for his wallet. Today, I was helping Mom do some online banking, and as I was looking at the credit card statement, I realized how right she was. There were several charities that Daddy donated to on a monthly basis, including the ASPCA, a Native American school in South Dakota, and WWF (World Wildlife Fund).

Mom wanted to take two walks instead of our usual one. Her leg hurt, but walking seems to be the only thing that gives her a bit of respite from the emptiness she feels at home. Only in New York City would a man walk around with a jockstrap over his face instead of a mask. When I saw him, I chuckled. In my head, I could hear Dad laughing and commenting loudly about the ridiculousness of it for everyone to hear.

Snapshot Rewind
1986: The summer before I turned twelve, Dad took us to Cape Cod for vacation. He rented a house in Eastham for two weeks. I remember the ocean being cold, so cold that only Dad and I went swimming. One day, we took a trip to Plymouth where we saw the *Mayflower* and we walked around Plimoth Plantation, a village recreated to show the first Pilgrim settlement. It's the first historical site my parents took me to on vacation. One day, I asked Dad if we could go to Boston as well. My sense of distance wasn't great. I figured we were in Massachusetts. Boston is in the same state. How far could it possibly be? The answer—too far. Which is why it

wasn't on Dad's itinerary for the summer. I was disappointed. In school, I had learned a bit about the Revolutionary War, and I wanted to see where the Boston Massacre and the Boston Tea Party took place.

Then one day, we woke up and it was raining. You can't go to the beach in the rain, so Dad announced we were going to Boston. I was excited. Once there, we walked the Freedom Trail, and it took us forever to find the site of the Boston Massacre. We expected some sort of monument that you could see from a distance. But it was just a plaque in the ground. We walked over it once or twice and then had to double back to find it. Along the way, we stopped at the *U.S.S. Constitution*—Old Iron Side—which had seen action in the War of 1812. On our tour of the ship, I asked the guide why America fought the War of 1812. He couldn't answer my question because he didn't know. I was so frustrated, and since it was decades before the internet, I couldn't look it up. It was years before I got an answer: Impressment, or forcing American merchant sailors to joint the Royal Navy, restrictions on trade in Europe, and conflict regarding westward expansion and relations with Native Americans.

From Dad, I developed a love of going on vacation and traveling to new places. From both of my parents, I learned to love and appreciate history so much that in many ways the two—travel and history—became intertwined. Now, whenever we go away on a family trip, I make sure we visit the historical sites along the way. It wouldn't be a real vacation if we didn't.

DAY 45

APRIL 29, 2020

I drove out to Mattituck with Mom because she wants to sell Dad's car back to the dealership in Riverhead. It's the first time in I-can't-remember-how-long that I arrived and Daddy wasn't here. In the before, as soon as he heard my car in the driveway, he'd rush out onto the porch to greet me and my son. But today, the house was empty and cold. This used to be my happy place, the home I ran away to when I was absolutely miserable. It cheered me up, it gave me strength. Not today. Today, it made me cry because the house alone is just a structure of wood filled with furniture. Without Dad, the happiness is gone.

Dad will never do anything with me ever again. He will never come back. Other people are complaining about how miserable they are because they are locked down in their homes. But someday, they will be able to step outside and resume their normal lives. Not me. When this pandemic ends, I will have to find my way in a whole new world. When others are celebrating, I'll still be crying. For me, my son, and my mother, this nightmare will never end. It will follow us forever. Every time we go somewhere or do something, we will be haunted by the thought, "I wish Daddy were here." Or "Daddy used to like this." Or "Remember how much fun you and Grandpa used to have?" I will carry the bitterness and sorrow with me forever.

Being here is hard. I am surrounded by memories. The last time I was here was back in November. I came to rake leaves. I always came in November to help with the leaves because Dad was getting old and it was exhausting. It hurt his back. Raking was the least I could do to help him, to give something back. I thought I'd be raking leaves for him for many years to come. I was wrong.

While being in this house is painful, I'm sure it's worse for Mom. She always used to joke, "This is your dad's house. The city house is mine." This is where Dad, like me, was happiest. After Dad retired, he and Mom used to come out here frequently. They went out to dinner. They enjoyed going to the movies. And many mornings they'd go out for breakfast and sip their coffee while enjoying each other's company. Since Mom doesn't drive, she can't come out unless I take her. She's already talking about selling it. "The house needs constant care and upkeep. I don't think I can do it without your father." Maybe she is right. If I beg her to keep it, am I being selfish?

Summers will have to enter a new era, but I'm not ready to leave the old one behind. My son and I came out here every summer for long stretches of time. It was the only thing that made living in New Jersey tolerable: the knowledge that I didn't have to live there all summer. I'd wake up early in the morning so that I could get over the bridges before traffic got too bad. When my son was a baby, and then a toddler, I'd gently pick him up out of bed and transfer him into the car. When he got older, I'd wake him so that he could use the bathroom and say goodbye to my spouse, but he never changed out of his pajamas. Even last summer, he didn't bother to put on shoes. Dad died before my son got too big for me to carry him from his room to my car.

Once here, when my son was little, Dad would pick him up out of the car and carry him inside. This house was my son's palace. Dad treated him like a king. Always, Dad was looking for fun things to share with my son. He'd take him fishing, to summer programs at the library, and to play miniature golf. In the fall, we went apple picking and pumpkin picking. My son only had to mention something, and Dad found a way to do it. One summer, my son wanted a giant blow-up alligator for the water. Of course, Dad bought it for him. Anything, as long as he was happy.

Greenport was one of my son's favorite places to go with Dad. He had a set routine that always included getting ice cream, going on the carousel, and stopping at the toy store so Dad could buy rubber ducks—my son must have fifty or more in his collection. When my son was really little, Dad would go on the carousel with him to hold him, to make sure he didn't fall off his horse. When he got older, Dad rode next to him, the cowboy and his sidekick. The last few times, Mom and Dad would sit and watch my son as he went on one ride after another, always reaching for the brass ring.

But most of our time was spent at the beach. When we came home, we'd take turns showering outside. I remember when my son graduated from the bathtub to the outdoor shower. He was about three. Too young to shower alone. So I'd keep my bathing suit on and wash him. Once he was clean, he'd scream as loudly as he could, "Bah-Bap." And Dad would come get him. He'd pull open the door, spread a towel wide, wrap it around his grandson, and carry him into the house.

In the mornings, sometimes my son would come into my room if he woke up before me. I'd pull him into a hug and hold him tight, prompting him to call Grandpa to save him. Grandpa always came, and we'd have a tug of war. Dad and I pulling my son while he laughed. Eventually, I'd let go, allowing Grandpa to rescue him. Other mornings, my son would wake up and go into his grandparents' room. He'd wiggle between them, and Dad would put on whatever cartoons he wanted to watch. Daddy loved those morning cuddles.

When we got to the house, the heat wasn't working, so Mom called to get someone to fix it. After they came, I went out for a walk. I headed down to the sound. The last time I was there was back in August. We went to watch the sunset. It was my son's idea, his request one night after dinner. My family was whole and happy, and when I took a picture of my son with his grandparents, his arms were around his grandfather's neck. He was happy.

I walked along the beach, but it was cold, cloudy, and windy—raw. Very raw. It's as if Dad went into the hospital in March, and the calendar got stuck, never progressing into April. Spring has been cold and rainy, as if it also misses my dad.

I want to know where the reset button is. How can I turn back the clock? Prevent my parents from going away? Keep them safe? Mom told me that the last few days on the boat, Dad was starting to worry. And Dad never worried. According to Mom, "He had his cell phone. He probably knew things were getting bad. And he grew anxious to get home." If only he never left—if only Trump had told the truth—I'd still have him here with me. My son would be happy. And I could deal with the boredom of a lockdown because this is where we were all supposed to be. Two weeks after my parents came home, we were supposed to come out here to weather the pandemic storm together. But we never got here. The virus claimed Dad before we could be with each other one final time.

We probably should have picked up water at Costco. We can't drink tap water here; it's not safe. When I pulled open the cabinet to see how many bottles we had, I thought of all the times Dad poked fun at how much water I drink. Before I'd come to visit, he'd tell Mom, "Liz is coming to visit. We should get more water." Dad used to make fun of me all the time. Always in jest. Sometimes, I was too sensitive. I wish I hadn't been. I should have just laughed along with him. But I didn't realize my days of laughing with him would come to such an abrupt end.

For school, my son had to write a haiku. His poem made me cry.

Murderous

Coronavirus
Like a serial killer
Killing everyone

Snapshot Rewind
1996: After graduating college, two friends and I drove cross country. At the end of our three-week trip, they dropped me off back home in Queens late at night. It was the day before Father's Day. Instead of going to bed, I got into my own car, and I drove out to Long Island. I wanted to surprise Dad. It was after midnight when I pulled into the driveway. Quietly, I crept into the house, and I fell asleep almost immediately. In the morning, Dad's voice, a tentative whisper as he stood by my door, woke me up. "Liz, is that you?" Groggy, I slid out of bed, smiled, and gave him a hug.

"Happy Father's Day."

DAY 46

APRIL 30, 2020

I'm in bed listening to the rain tap down on the roof. It's one of those sounds that used to lull me to sleep. Not today. I'm so tired, but I haven't been able to sleep well since Dad went into the hospital. Yesterday, in the news, they announced that the HIV drug, Remdesivir, has proven to help severely sick coronavirus patients recover. The doctors wouldn't give the drug to my dad because of his secondary infection. They said it would be too hard on his body. But since the alternative was death, I still don't understand why they didn't at least try. What if it could have saved him? What if it could have brought him home?

I knew being in this house would be hard, but I think it's even harder than I expected. My parents' room is next to mine. My bed and their bed are pressed up against opposite sides of the same wall. Whenever I slept here, I could hear both Mom and Dad snoring all night, every night. And it was loud, but I had become so accustomed to it that the quiet is unsettling. Even Mom isn't snoring because she won't sleep in her bed, even here. She slept in the living room, sitting partially upright in the reclining chair. When I asked her why, she explained, "It's too lonely. I'll miss your father even more." After almost fifty years of sharing a bed, I suppose sleeping alone would be unsettling. The bed would feel too big.

We used to call this house the "country house," until my son, as a toddler, started to refer to it as the "beach house." There was Nonna and Grandpa's "city house" and their "beach house." That's how he differentiated them. But when people hear beach house, they think oceanfront property and big house. So it can be a bit deceiving. The house is tiny, but cozy—one floor, three little bedrooms, a large living room with a small dining room table next to a decent-sized kitchen. A closet-sized bathroom is off to the side as if it were once upon a time tacked on as an afterthought. The house is not on the water, but the Long Island Sound is within walking distance. And the bay, which is where we usually swim because the beach isn't as rocky, is about three miles away.

My parents bought this house, I think, when I was a senior in high school. When they bought it, it was falling to pieces. They had to hire a construction guy to completely renovate the inside. He also added a deck out back, as well as an outdoor shower. Dad had been very insistent about an outdoor shower. I don't know why. But over the years, painting it with water sealant became my job, one I did almost every summer, including last year. Shortly after they bought the house, we came out one weekend to do some work on it. Mom was going to work in the kitchen, and Dad planned to clean up the yard. Mom asked me to help her, and Dad intended to take my brother outside. However, my brother and I exchanged one brief look, and he stayed to help Mom and I went with Dad. I preferred being outside. I still do.

The week of my senior spring break, Mom and I came out here together. There was still lots of work outside to be done. Years worth of leaves had collected, and they had to be raked. Branches had fallen and needed to be picked up. It was tedious work, but I have always enjoyed that kind of mindless, rhythmic outdoor labor. I had only recently gotten my driver's license, so Dad was nervous about lending me the car to drive out here. He told me I was only permitted to drive in the right lane, and I was not to go so much as one mile per hour over the speed limit. The entire drive I clutched the wheel—hands precisely at ten and two—fretting about going too fast, worried when I needed to switch lanes in order to follow signs and go the right way. It was the most nerve-wracking drive of my life, but we arrived safely.

After I graduated high school, I got my very first job working at the local movie theater. It was great because I was allowed to let friends and family members into the movies for free. Dad, as you know, loved the movies, and so I invited him and Mom all the time. He must have seen at least one movie a week that summer, if not more. And not only were his movies free, but the popcorn was as well. It may have been the only time in my life that I had the opportunity to spoil him. They would arrive at the theater, I'd wave them in and then hand them a brown paper bag—the kind I used to use for my lunch in high school—filled with popcorn.

The following summer, I got a job selling parking passes for the town at the local beaches. I had that job for three summers. Five days a week, I'd sit in the parking lot down by the bay in New Suffolk. On days when Dad wasn't working, he and Mom would come to the beach where I worked. During my lunch break, I'd go sit with my parents. We'd eat together and then we'd go for a swim. When it wasn't busy, and New Suffolk wasn't one of the busy beaches, Dad would come up to me with the beach paddle ball game and we'd play for a while. On occasion, my boss sent me to Sound Beach off the North Road out in Southold. It was farther from home and much more crowded, but sometimes my parents drove out there if it was where I was working. I was never that teenager that didn't want to spend time with my parents. It was a phase I never went through.

This morning, Mom and I got bagels for breakfast, and we drove to the bay to eat them. We sat in the car in the parking lot. It was cold and windy—though the rain had stopped. The bay, which is usually calm, was stormy. Waves crashed on the sand and white-caps rippled up from the water. Mom and Dad often used to drive to the beach for breakfast. On warm days, they'd sit outside at one of the picnic tables, but on the cooler or rainy days, they'd sit in the car, sip their coffee, and look out at the water.

We're back in Queens. To sell Dad's car to the dealership, it turns out Mom needs the lien release form along with the title (which we had with us), so we had to drive back to the city to find it. If all goes well, we'll sell the car on Saturday. Mom doesn't want to get rid of it because it was Dad's, and there are so many memories attached to it, but she doesn't drive. To hold onto it and pay insurance would be foolish. I offered to teach her how to drive, but she claims to be too old. She's too afraid of hurting someone or killing them on the road.

My memory on Facebook made me both smile and cry. Seven years ago, I posted, "Gary talked Grandpa into carrying him home from the playground on his shoulders. Walking home he looked down at me and said, 'I higher than Mama. I can see the whole world.'" Grandpa lifted him up in so many ways. And in taking him places, and doing things with him, he had showed him the world. Only he wasn't finished. There was so much more Dad wanted to do with my son, so much more of the world he wanted to show him.

Snapshot Rewind
Sometime in the mid-1990s: Daddy and Fireball loved taking walks on the beach. When I was with them in Long Island, I always joined them because I also like walking. Though it was their company I enjoyed more. One afternoon, either late winter or early spring, the three of us got in my car, and I drove to our favorite bay

beach in Peconic. Years later, my son would refer to it as the Treasure Beach, but that's a story for another time. Anyway, while we were walking—on the beach in the off-season we never kept Fireball on a leash—Fireball spotted a flock of seagulls hanging out in the water. She took off in a sprint after them. Despite Dad and I both calling her, she got to the edge of the water, leaped into the air, and landed with a splash, scattering the birds in a whirlwind of feathers and screeches. Dad roared with laughter. I fumed over the fact that I was going to have to bring a wet dog home in my new car. I hadn't even brought a towel for her to sit on or to dry her off with. It was cold. No one was supposed to have gone swimming. I was in a bad mood for the rest of the walk, and Dad's laughter only made me crankier. But in years to come, I'd learn to see the humor. Dad and I would reminisce about it and laugh together.

DAY 47

MAY 1, 2020

Daddy had a terrible childhood. His father was an alcoholic and a mean drunk. His mother—Dad felt—cared only for herself. When Dad was little, his mother put him to bed every night by six o'clock, not because he needed sleep, but because if he was awake when his drunk father came home, his father would beat him. Dad grew up in a house of violence, one in which he felt unloved. I've read how abused children tend to grow up and abuse their own kids, but that wasn't Dad. It's almost as if Dad had been taking notes all through his childhood about the things he wanted, the things he wished he had, so that when he grew up and became a father, he could give his kids all the things he once wanted.

His first memory was of the day the family's first television was delivered. He was two years old, but the memory remained crisp in his mind. From the moment it entered his house, Dad loved watching it. His favorite shows were *Davey Crockett* and *Daniel Boone*. He loved his coonskin cap and pretending that he lived on the frontier. When he was four years old, he also had a cowboy outfit and a toy gun that he really liked. Escape. I suppose that's what television was for Dad—a way to be someone else, if only for a half hour. As I write, I wonder if this is where Dad's interest in history was born. Did he grow up to like visiting historical sites and reading historic fiction because of these early televisions shows?

When Dad was a kid, his family would go on vacation to Welcome Lake in Pennsylvania. Vacation usually coincided with Dad's birthday—July 16. What Dad remembered most was that he never had a birthday party with his friends. His parents would have a party for him at the lake, but it was always with strangers, kids he didn't know. It never really felt special, and that always bothered him. Maybe that's why, as an adult, doing something fun and having his family around for his birthday was so important to him. We always tried to visit on or near his birthday, and one year, not long ago, my son made him a homemake birthday cake and iced it to look like a baseball. Oh, how dad appreciated that cake. His smile said it all.

Sometime in elementary school—Sacred Heart, the same school I attended—maybe in second grade, Daddy got in trouble for kissing a girl. The principal sent him home and told him he couldn't come back to school unless his mother returned with him. His mother wasn't happy, but she brought him to school, and Dad went back to class with no further punishment. That was one of the few stories Dad ever told me about his childhood. I wish I had asked him to tell me more, but whenever I tried to bring it up, he seemed to shut down.

My grandmother was racist. When Dad was young, she'd occasionally take him to the five-and-dime and buy him an egg cream. But she always made him hold the handle with his left hand. The thought of his lips touching the same spot on the glass as an African American's repulsed her. This story that Dad told me more than once—even as a young child—was my first introduction to racism. And the way Dad told it, it was clear that he believed his mother's words and actions were wrong. He'd add with a smile, "It's like it never occurred to her that a Black person could be left-handed."

Dad joined Cub Scouts. It was something he really wanted to do. But he didn't participate for long because his mother refused to buy him a uniform. He was the only boy who didn't have one, and he felt left out. I guess that's why he wanted his son and his grandson to participate in scouts. He felt he had missed out on an incredible opportunity and he wanted that for the other Garys.

In school, when he wasn't kissing girls, Dad did very well academically. He was smart enough that somewhere along the way, he skipped a grade. When he graduated from Bishop Loughlin Memorial High School, he was only sixteen years old. He was always very proud of that.

His parents refused to pay for him to go to college, so he went to City College of New York, which, at the time, was free. However, his senior year, the campus he attended became Baruch College. As a result, his diploma reads Baruch, not CCNY, which always bothered him. He always resented having to attend a CUNY school. He wanted to go to a better college, perhaps study something in the medical field, but his parents' lack of support forced him to study business instead. It wasn't what he wanted, and he wasn't happy. As a result, my "A" student father barely passed college with Cs. He vowed that his kids would go to the best universities they could get into, regardless of the cost. So he paid for me to attend New York University. He also paid for me to live in a dorm even though I could have easily commuted. He paid for my brother to attend Johns Hopkins University. He could have retired earlier. He could have enjoyed more years of traveling with Mom, but first he had to pay off the money he borrowed against his pension so that his children could be well educated.

A cousin once asked me if I knew how my father overcame his awful upbringing. He died before I could ask him. But if I had to guess, it had to do with wanting more for his family than he ever had. He once told me that he always wished he had a grandfather. Sometimes I think he was such a fantastic grandfather because he gave my son the relationship he always wanted, the connection he craved and never had. Maybe it was like that every step of the way. He didn't have a good relationship with his parents, so he wanted to make sure he had one with me.

Mom didn't sleep at all last night. Yesterday, she heard on the news that back on April 9th, the former Fox News host, Bill O'Reilly, offensively commented that people who died from COVID-19 "were on their last legs anyway." What a cruel and heartless thing to say, but what more can you expect from a Fox guy? He said it before Dad died, when Dad was still fighting for his life. But Dad certainly wasn't on his last legs. He was healthy—for a seventy-one-year-old man. He had just come back from vacation. He could still drive. His mind was sharp. There was nothing back in February to indicate that he could die soon. And then one insensitive asshole makes a vicious comment that not only insults my dead father, it also hurts my mother so much that she sat awake all night in more pain than she had been in. This morning—the comment still echoing in her mind—she's been crying almost continuously. It's bad enough that Trump's lies and incompetence killed my dad. Now his supporters think it's okay to disrespect the dead and further hurt the living. Trump's America is not an America I respect, nor one that anyone with any sense of decency should have any pride in.

I took Mom grocery shopping today. As we were leaving and getting into the elevator, she said, "Even coming here is miserable. Your father and I used to come here all the time, and all I can think about is how he used to joke about everything." Her laughter seems to have died with Dad.

This evening, my son and my spouse came to New York. I need my spouse's help tomorrow to sell Dad's car. I can't drop the car off if I don't have someone to drive me home. They got here in time for dinner, and after we ate, Mom, my spouse, and I continued to sit at the table where we talked about Dad. With a bottle of wine on the table and our glasses full, we took turns telling stories. For the first time in days, Mom smiled and even laughed a little, though a sadness lingered behind her smile.

Dad was cremated today. He died seventeen days ago. That's how badly death has affected New York City. It took more than two weeks for a spot to open up for his body. This morning, the funeral home piled many coffins into a truck to drive to a crematorium in Connecticut. They had to cross state lines because the crematoriums in New York are overrun. Just writing these words makes me feel hollow inside. Daddy is dead. All that remains are my memories.

Snapshot Rewind

July 15, 2018: My son doesn't play baseball. I enrolled him in tee-ball when he was four and again when he was five, but he didn't love it. Baseball just didn't interest him, and I was never going to push it. But Dad loved baseball, and he was a die-hard Mets fan. I don't think he ever missed a game whether he listened to it on the radio—I have so many memories of sitting in beach traffic as a kid coming home from Jones Beach and listening to baseball games—or watched it on television. My son knew that Dad loved the Mets, and two years ago, he asked Grandpa to take him to a baseball game.

Of course, Dad said yes. He sent me the dates of several afternoon games, asking me to pick the one that would work best. We settled on July 15th, the day before Dad's birthday. Dad reserved tickets online, good seats on the first base line. The morning of the game, the boys left early so Dad could take my son out for breakfast at the diner in Riverhead—we were staying at the Mattituck house. When they arrived at City Field, Dad arranged for my son to participate in all the pregame activities for kids, and they had their picture taken with Mr. Met. Dad bought my son a baseball cap, the expensive one, because when it came to his grandson, money was never a question. He spent it freely, happily. During the game, my son ate a sundae in a small plastic helmet.

The Mets lost.

When they got home, I asked Dad if my son behaved. And he had—beautifully. But my son always behaved best for Grandpa.

Last summer, in late August, they went to another game. They enjoyed going to the first one so much that they couldn't wait to go again. This time, Dad bought them matching Alonso shirts. He bought my son one that was too big so that he could grow into it, so that they could wear it the following year when they went to another game. That was always the plan, and while Dad was in South America, my son said to me, "I can't wait to go to a baseball game this summer with Grandpa. When he comes back, I'm going to make sure he gets tickets."

Mom offered to give me money so that I could take him to a game when the world opens up again, but he won't want to go with me. I know too well that it was never about baseball. It was about a special boys' day with the grandpa he adored.

DAY 48

MAY 2, 2020

Every day I miss Daddy more. I still can't believe this happened to me. To my family. I still can't believe this is the reality in which I am living, the reality in which I need to acclimate. How could he be here one moment and dead the next? And to think, the last real conversation I had with him—the Wednesday before I took him to the hospital—ended in an argument about politics.

My Dad used to be a Republican. Until he died, I referred to him as a Reagan Republican. He thought Reagan was one of the best presidents America ever had. I strongly disagreed, but whenever I tried to argue the point, Dad would get mad and end the conversation with, "I hardly paid taxes when Reagan was president. My take-home salary enabled me to do more for you and your brother." And that was Dad. He had to be right—always. Which meant sometimes it was easier to let things go because I knew I'd never change his mind anyway. So when it came to Reagan, I stopped trying. It was history, after all, and neither of us were going to change it, so why fight over it?

Dad stopped being a devout Republican when Baby Bush ran for president. I remember sitting at the dinner table on Election Day and him telling me that he voted for Gore. But he couldn't quite bring himself to vote for the Democratic Party, so he voted for Gore under the Working Man's Party. After that, Dad became an Independent. In local elections, he would sometimes still vote for a Republican, but never again would he cast his vote for a Republican running for president. He liked Obama, and while he wasn't a fan of Hillary Clinton, he did vote for her because he detested Trump. After Trump was elected, Dad and I often made fun of him. At least, we made fun of his stupidity when we weren't furious at him over his racist and elitist policies.

When it came to Trump, Dad and I were united. But I lean further left on the political spectrum than Dad did. During the primary, we backed very different candidates. He liked Biden and then Bloomberg. I was partial to Sanders. Dad hated the idea of socialism. He grew up during the Cold War, so I suppose it's not that hard to understand. During that era, anything that hinted at communism was evil, even socialism which is not synonymous with communism. However, where I'm standing, I see, not socialism but unrestrained capitalism as the problem. In our very last conversation, I asked Dad what he planned to do with Trump's stimulus check if he got one. After all, the government giving out money was a socialist move. But the question angered Dad, and he snapped at me. "I'll use the money to help pay off your car. So I don't want to hear any complaining from you." I wasn't complaining, but Dad had that tone, that look in his eyes (we were FaceTiming) that said, either you can agree with me or drop it. I dropped it. What a waste. Our last real conversation and it had to be a disagreement over something so stupid.

Today was a crappy day. Actually, the last thirty-six days have been crappy, so I suppose at this point I shouldn't expect more. We drove out to Long Island with the intention of selling Dad's car back to the Toyota dealership where he bought it, but things did not go well.

When Mom first called the dealership, she spoke to a guy named Chris. She told him the whole story about Dad dying and the car being in his name only, as well as the fact that she didn't drive so she had to get rid of it. He told her to bring the car in with the title. "Just the title, nothing else?" Mom asked, wanted to make sure. He said no, *just the title*. We did as we were told, but when we got there, Chris told us we also needed the lien release paperwork. Mom was angry, furious that he had not been honest and thorough, but what could she do, other than agree to come back with the required paperwork.

This morning, Mom called again to make sure Chris would be there and to ask one more time what paperwork she needed. He repeated that all she needed was the lien release and the title. My spouse drove in from New Jersey yesterday so that she could come to the dealership with us. After breakfast, we drove to Riverhead. When we arrived at the dealership, Chris said he'd be out in five minutes. A half-hour later, he emerged. He looked at the title, told Mom to sign it, and then said, "Oh wait, I can't take this. Your husband has to sign it."

We—I, Mom, and my spouse—looked at him and said, "But he's dead."

Chris shrugged. "Well then you need the death certificate and certified proof that you are the power of attorney."

Mom started to cry. "But I asked you several times what I needed, and the death certificate never came up."

Now Chris was just being an asshole. "You must have spoken to someone else." No, Mom only spoke to him. No one else. But he didn't care that the fact that he wasn't paying attention cost us a drive we didn't need to make. That he angered an already overwhelmed widow. Like everyone else in this fucking pandemic who hasn't lost a loved one, it was just business as usual. I'm so god-damn tired of the fact that so few people have any compassion at all. I can't tell you how many calls and conversations Mom and I have had these last three weeks, and only two people in the business world, two—Wilma at Express Scripts and John at Capital One—have expressed any kindness or compassion at all.

Angry, and feeling completely taken advantage of, Mom got back into Dad's car and cried some more. We drove out to the house in Mattituck, had lunch, and then headed over to Veterans Beach to take a short stroll along the bay. We walked down to the inlet. Mom looked so small and stooped and sad walking without Dad. They used to hold hands all the time. I always thought they'd grow really old together, still holding hands, still doing everything with each other. But life rarely turns out as we envision it, as we hope and pray it will. Without Dad's hand to hold her up, Mom almost looked like she was sinking into the sand.

At the inlet, we stopped and sat on the bulkhead. It feels so weird being at the beach without Dad. He and I went kayaking there a few times, into the inlet to explore the channels. We took countless walks on the beach with my son. My son sketched a jellyfish in the wet sand, and we reminisced about the time—my son was only four—when my dad took several red jellyfish out of the water so they wouldn't sting anyone. My son was extremely impressed that Dad could touch the red jellyfish and not get hurt. He thought he was a superhero. But what some people don't know, and what my son hadn't yet learned, is that the palm of your hand is not suscep-tible to jellyfish stings. About a week ago, my memory on Facebook was a throwback to when my son had commented: "Last summer, Grandpa was so brave. He took all the red jellyfish out of the water and covered them with sand. Everyone on the beach was then safe to go into the water."

I am now back in Queens with Mom and my son. My spouse went home to New Jersey, where my son and I will join her tomorrow.

Snapshot Rewind

1993: When I was born, my parents opened a bank account for me. Every birthday, Christmas, or sacrament, when I got money as a gift, I'd hand it directly to Dad, and he would deposit it in my account. I knew I had money. I knew I wasn't allowed to spend it when I got it. But I had no idea how much there was. When I got to college, I wanted a car. Not for school, obviously. You don't need a car when you go to college in Manhattan. I wanted one for the summer so I could drive around Long Island, go out with friends, and drive to work. When I told my dad I wanted a car, he gave me access to my bank account so I could buy one. All those years of saving money had paid off.

Dad drove me to the Toyota dealership in Riverhead. I didn't have enough money for a new car, but a gently used one would do. There was a shiny red Nissan sports car that both Dad and I liked, so I bought it. I paid for the car with my money, but Dad insisted on getting and paying for an extended warranty. It was a used car, and he wanted to make sure it would last, that in the end, it would be worth the money I spent.

I had that car until graduate school. Again, I went to New York University, and a car in Manhattan wasn't necessary. Since my parents had the foresight to save my money instead of allowing me to spend it frivolously as I got it, I not only had the pleasure of buying a car when I wanted one, but I then sold it and had the money to pay for one semester of graduate school.

How I paid for the rest of that degree is another story for another day.

DAY 49

MAY 3, 2020

"I knew something bad was going to happen," Mom said as we were driving home from Long Island yesterday. "Things happen in threes. Aunt Annamarie died. Then Aunt Mickey. I knew death was coming, I just didn't expect it to be your father." No one expected it to be him. I never would have guessed, three months ago, that this year would make me fatherless.

This morning, my son wanted to cuddle. "I miss Grandpa, so you have to cuddle with me." I couldn't say no. Cuddles make me feel a little better, too.

After breakfast, we headed back to New Jersey. It was a beautiful, warm spring day, a day that made it impossible to stay indoors. Governor Murphy reopened state and county parks yesterday, so we decided to go for a family hike—a much-needed family day. On the way to Schooley's Mountain, we stopped at Panera and picked up a late lunch—soup, sandwiches, and bread. When we got to the park, we found a picnic table far enough away from other people, and we sat down to eat.

As I've already mentioned, my son doesn't dress like most kids. Instead of comfortable clothes, or what I would consider comfortable clothes, he wore jeans, a white button-down short-sleeved shirt, and a vest, along with a straw hat. He looked more like he was heading to church than going into the woods. We hadn't been hiking long when we reached a stream stretching out from the base of a waterfall. My son insisted on stopping, taking off his boots, and putting his feet in the water. We all did. It was cold but refreshing, and my son was smiling. It's the happiest I have seen him in a really long time. I guess we all needed a break from the pandemic. From our grief. But the longer we sat on the rocks, talking and listening to the water from the falls crashing into the stream, the more my mind began to drift to Dad. How can I not think of him? If he were still alive, I'd have taken a picture of my son and texted it to him. Whenever we went on vacation or took a day trip, I'd send him pictures of my son to let him know we were thinking of him. Just getting a picture of his grandson made him happy.

While I sat on a rock, my feet soaking in the stream, I thought back to when Mom and Dad took us to Shenandoah during our family vacation back in 1987. I loved staying in the park. The cabins were rustic and quaint, in my opinion. Mom and Dad thought they were musty and run-down. But I felt very much at home. Like I belonged in the woods. While there, we met another family, and the seven of us set out on a hike one afternoon. The adults planned for it to be a short hike, but somewhere along the way, we followed the wrong blaze and ended up going a much longer distance. I didn't mind. I was happy. Perhaps the wrong blaze was my fault because I've always preferred longer and harder when it comes to hiking.

That was the same summer we went to Williamsburg, another historical site that I enjoyed. I remember once, I'm not sure if it was that summer or another, but I thanked Dad for taking me on vacation. He smiled and said, "You never have to say thank you. But when you have a child, I expect you to do the same for him or her." That stayed with me all these years. Every time I take my son somewhere new, I hear my dad in the back of my head repeating those words.

Last night, I mentioned to Mom that before the pandemic canceled all our plans, we had intended to visit Niagara Falls this coming summer. Mom glanced over at my son, then turned back to me. "It made your father very happy when you took your son on vacation. It made him happier to know that you appreciated our trips so much you wanted to recreate them with your own kid."

I chuckled. "I guess copying someone is the best compliment."

Mom nodded. "You made your father proud."

We had a good day until we sat down to eat dinner. My son asked to watch a movie, but it was late, and the movie he wanted to watch would not have ended until eleven. When we said no, he fell apart—crying, screaming, hitting things. There was no calming him. My spouse sent him to bed, but he refused to move. His screams grew louder. He shouted that we were terrible parents, that we didn't love him, that we didn't cook good meals for him, that one of us should have died instead of Grandpa. "Grandpa loved me. Grandpa loved me more than anyone. And now he's gone." My son sat down on the stairs, his entire body slumped, his head pressed into his hands. "I want him back. I want him back. I just want him back." My spouse and I sat down next to him, one on either side, and pulled him into a hug. He whimpered, "I want him back."

"I know," I cried with him. "I want him back, too."

Finally, my son calmed down. He brushed his teeth, went to bed, and the fucking police knocked on our door. One of my asshole neighbors called in a domestic violence complaint. I have never known rage like I did in that moment. My son is in pain because the man he loved most died, and instead of being compassionate, my neighbors are complete pricks. And the cops are no better. They had the audacity to show up without wearing masks. How fucking rude can they be? I have absolutely no respect for cops. If you show up at my house during a pandemic without a mask, you don't deserve respect. Seeing the anger blazing in my eyes and hearing vitriol spewing from my mouth, my spouse pushed me inside to deal with the cops by herself. I suppose that was best.

Snapshot Rewind

Circa 1985: Mom and Dad took us up to Lake Placid for a few days during our February break. It was the first time I went downhill skiing. I wasn't very good. We also went cross-country skiing which I very much enjoyed. Like the hike in Shenandoah, we intended to take a short route, nothing too far. But also like in Virginia, we ended up on the wrong path and went much farther than intended. I was happy to stay out longer on the trail because I thought cross-country skiing was much more fun than downhill skiing. Perhaps it's because I felt I had more control. By the time we finished, Mom, Dad, and my brother were exhausted.

Walking through the town was always enjoyable, and there was one restaurant that I distinctly remember eating in because I really liked the French onion soup. However, the most memorable experience was our ride on the Olympic bobsled. We had gotten to the complex late, and there were only two tickets left. Of course, Dad bought them for me and my brother, since it was more important to him that we got to go. He was happy to see us have a good time. I remember racing down the course, the wind in my face and my head—it's a good thing we had to wear helmets—smashing against the side of the sled every time we turned.

"How was it?" Dad asked as we climbed out of the sled.

"Great." And it was, but everything we did on vacation was great. I just loved being away and being with my family. I guess some things never change.

DAY 50

MAY 4, 2020

I didn't sleep at all last night. I was too angry. On top of everything else, I didn't need to deal with cops. I can't believe they weren't even wearing face masks, nor did they stand six feet away from us. They showed no regard for our health. If I'm required to wear a face mask when going grocery shopping, cops should be required to wear a mask when knocking on my door. At least one Bedminster cop died from COVID-19; that indicates to me that the cops who showed up could also have been exposed. Infected. They can very easily be carrying the virus, and I resent their callousness. Their unwillingness to follow proper CDC protocol. Cops should not be above the law or the rules set into place to keep people safe. I've said before that I'm falling apart. Dad didn't deserve death. Mom and my son didn't deserve the fallout from his death—the pain and anger and unbearable sadness. I can barely get up most days, and then I come home for *one* day—one fucking day—and I'm harassed by neighbors and police.

Yesterday, before the cops arrived, I got an email saying that my essay about my honeymoon in Costa Rica was accept for publication. However, the editors want me to revise the ending. They want something stronger. I wasn't sure what I could add, so I asked my spouse if she had any suggestions. She reminded me of the awful storm we had to drive through on our last night. The rain pelting the windshield, making it nearly impossible to see the road. Thinking that might work well as an ending, I wrote about it for the last vignette of the essay.

This morning, I found out that my short travel essay recounting my visit to Hans Christian Andersen's house in Denmark has also been accepted for publication—by a different journal. That's two essays accepted in two days. It's almost as if Daddy is somewhere whispering in editors' ears, telling them to pick me. Maybe now would be a good time to start sending out query letters again for my novels and essay collections. Perhaps Dad really is somewhere that he can continue to look out for me. But I still wish he were here. I still wish I could call him up or tag him on Facebook with the good news. I want, just one more time, to hear him say, "Very nice." It's what he said all the time, regardless of what I did or the extent of my accomplishment. If I posted a pretty picture on Facebook, he commented, "Very nice." If I published an essay or short story, he said, "Very nice." When I graduated from grad school, he hugged me and exclaimed, "Very nice." And I used to get so upset when he said those words because they seemed bland, so void of emotion. Nice, I felt, was a word one used when they didn't have something better—more meaningful—to offer. Now, I'd give anything to hear him say it. I wish I hadn't been so critical. I wish I had accepted his compliments.

My brother is driving up from Nashville. He is going to spend some time with Mom and take her up to his condo in Cape Cod. Since he'll be there late tonight or early tomorrow, I thought it would be good to spend some time with my son, just the two of us. He's felt pushed aside since Dad got sick. I'm hoping some concentrated attention will make him feel a little better, or at least a little less rebellious. After he completed his schoolwork for the day, we drove out to Mattituck. Our favorite place.

I considered driving out to Mattituck this morning, but the thought of getting there early and not having Dad to greet us, not having Dad to make us breakfast, was too sad. So we left at two-thirty. Back before the pandemic struck, I never would have considered leaving at such an absurd time—the heart of rush hour. Traffic would have killed me. But there is no rush hour, nor is there traffic. I stopped for gas in Jersey—$1.85 a gallon—and I still made better time than I used to make leaving at five-thirty in the morning. It feels weird being here—just the two of us. It's like part of me expects Mom and Dad to walk in at any moment. Still, it's far more peaceful than being in Bedminster. My body doesn't shake as much, and I don't feel as tightly wound.

When we arrived, we ate dinner, and then my son wanted to work on another puzzle. After it got dark, we went out back, sat on the deck, and watched the meteor shower for a short while until my son got cold and wanted to come back inside. Now, he is in bed, and an eeriness has settled over the house. It's not supposed to be this quiet. I'm supposed to hear the television in my parents' bedroom, or their snores—something other than the wind.

Snapshot Rewind
2010–2017: My son loved going to Long Island for a long weekend every fall. We'd go out around Nonna's birthday—October 19th—and Grandpa would spoil him, perhaps a little more than usual. Mom would buy him costumes—pirate, Batman, Spiderman—or masks and swords, and she'd put them on his bed so when he got there he'd see them and get excited. She bought them not for Halloween but because he enjoyed wearing costumes. He'd put one on, and Dad would take us apple picking and pumpkin picking. We picked more apples than we could possibly eat, and my son always took home a pumpkin along with several gourds. All he had to do was ask, and Grandpa would pay for whatever he wanted.

Spending a day in the play area at Harbes Farm was something that always excited my son. He'd ride the bikes, visit with the goats, play with the rubber duckies at the water pump, and jump in the bounce house. In between, he'd eat corn on the cob, which Dad bought at the farm stand, and play on the tractor. He loved pretending to drive it. His absolute favorite activity was walking through the corn maze which had a Sherwood Forest theme. We did it several years, but we—the adults—always got lost and frustrated that we couldn't find our way. My son never seemed to care. He'd push on. smiling, convinced he was going the correct way even though we knew we'd already tried that direction and would end up at a dead end. Shooting the arrows was always fun. But it was the end—when one person in each party got to sword fight against Robin Hood—that my son enjoyed most. He took it very seriously, and when he won, he believed he had saved us all.

DAY 51

MAY 5, 2020

When I was young, I had a collection of Hans Christian Andersen fairy tales. Mom and Dad would take turns, alternating nights, reading to me before bed. Mom warned Dad not to read me "The Red Shoes." It was terribly sad, and she didn't want me to cry, but I begged Dad to read it, and he did. Sure enough, by the end of the story, I was sobbing. Nothing Dad said could console me. When he asked Mom what he should do, she scolded him, "I told you not to read it to her." Hans Christian Andersen has always been one of my favorite storytellers, and the more his stories made me cry, the more I liked them. I suppose that element of sorrow and sadness is the reason I have always felt drawn to Andersen's stories. They didn't always end "happily ever after." They were realistic and, therefore, more relatable. So maybe I did get a fairy tale ending after all, only it was the Andersen variety, one that ended in death and brought tears to readers, like "The Little Match Girl" and "The Little Mermaid"—before Disney sabotaged the ending.

Years ago, in the winter of 2004, I visited Denmark for a week. My Dad's ancestry was partially Danish—or we always believed it was until he had his DNA tested and not a single drop of Dane showed up anywhere. His mother's maiden name was Rasmussen—one of the more common Danish surnames. I wanted to go to Denmark to see where my ancestors had come from—I had already visited Germany and Italy on prior trips—and to visit the childhood home of Hans Christian Andersen. I have always liked visiting the houses of famous dead people. Yes, it's the history and personal stories that I enjoy learning most, but also, sometimes, if I'm still enough and the sun hits the window just right, I can almost catch a glimpse of their essence, a ghostly encounter of sorts. Though it is fleeting, it's a way to connect with them through time.

To get to Hans' house, I had to travel by train from Copenhagen to Odense. But I've often said I live under a dark cloud, and that afternoon, the cloud was definitely present. I traveled all that way to discover that his house was closed for renovations. This was before easy internet access on smartphones, websites at your fingertips to give you updates on closings and other pertinent information, so I had no idea until I arrived. I was devastated. Like some of his stories, my adventure would end in disappointment. But at least there was a museum to explore, so it wasn't like I wasted my time completely.

Dad died three weeks ago. As of this morning, when I turned on the news, 69,000 Americans have died. That means 69,000 families are crushed, mourning the loss of a loved one. I am not alone. But now the president and his son-in-law are trying to rewrite the script regarding the death toll. In an interview last week—April 29—Jared Kushner said, "So, the government, federal government, rose to the challenge, and this is a great success story, and I think that that's really what needs to be told." Let me be clear: anything that involved the death of my father is *not* a success story. Anything that claimed more lives than Vietnam in a fraction of the time is *not* a success story. How can anyone look at the numbers and claim success? What Kushner and Trump need is a tour of the New York City cemeteries and crematoriums. They need to talk to the grave diggers and the families that are no longer whole. The families that have been left with nothing but memories of people they once cherished. They need to read this book. But they won't do any of that because they don't care about the people. That has been evident from the start. If they ignore the reality, the facts in front of them—

and we know Trump is exceptionally gifted at ignoring facts—they can make up any story they want. And that is exactly what they are doing. The super sad thing about it is many Americans will believe them because they, too, care more about money and superficial things, like eating out in a restaurant, than they care about human lives. My Dad—and 69,000 other people—is nothing more than a statistic to them. But to me, Dad was everything.

In contrast to Trump, Cuomo genuinely appears to care about the residents of New York. Since the beginning of this pandemic, since the moment Cuomo had a grasp of how horrific it is, he has done his best to combat it, to protect and save as many New Yorkers as possible. If Cuomo had the same intel Trump did back in January, Dad might not have died because Cuomo would have told the truth. And the truth, I believe, would have kept my father off that boat. But Cuomo is only a governor, not the president, so he doesn't have the same access to information, especially on the world's stage.

This afternoon, Governor Cuomo once again earned my respect when, unlike Trump, he emphasized the fact that he values people over money. He explained to New Yorkers, "The faster we re-open, the lower the economic cost—but the higher the human cost." It's a simple enough equation. Unfortunately, there are people out there who are willing to sacrifice more people for the sake of the economy. Cuomo made it clear that such an atrocity would not happen on his watch. "How much is a human life worth? That's the real discussion that no one has admitted openly and freely. But we should. To me, I say the most of human life—a human life is priceless." Yes, he, too, wants to reopen New York, but not if it means filling more cemetery plots.

I finally finished reading *Pale Rider*. It was published in 2017, only three years ago, and it ends with a warning that another pandemic will most definitely occur. At the time, scientists believed it would be another strand of the flu; the fact that it was something else does not excuse the president's inaction. Several agencies around the world—including the CDC—were tasked with monitoring for a future outbreak. They knew it was coming, but instead of ramping up surveillance, Trump disbanded the pandemic response team. According to Spinney on page 282,

"The media clearly have a critical role to play in any future pandemic, and 1918 taught us a valuable lesson in this too: censorship and playing down the danger don't work; relaying accurate information in an objective and timely fashion does. Information and engagement are not the same thing, however. Even when people have the information they need to contain the disease, they do not necessarily act on it."

There are many news stations that are currently trying to give us the truth, an accurate picture of what we need to know. Sadly, Trump continuously accuses them of being fake news. He doesn't like the truth because the truth makes him look like the bumbling, selfish idiot he is.

But let's look more closely at exactly what Spinney said. "Censorship and playing down the danger don't work." Thanks to the First Amendment, censorship is illegal. But Trump certainly did downplay the danger (see Day 37). He told us not to worry. He told us it was under control. He promised it would go away. He should have said, back in January, "The coronavirus has arrived in America. We can't control it. And it has the potential to kill you and/or your loved ones if you are not careful." But as Spinney pointed out, even when people have the necessary information, they do not act on it. And that is Trump's greatest fault. So, Kushner is absolutely wrong when he tries to portray this as a success story. Trump had the information, and for too long, he did nothing. His lack of action cost the lives of too many Americans. His apathy robbed my son of his grandfather.

After reading the news this evening, it looks like Trump is determined to rob more children of their grandparents. In an interview with ABC News, he once again emphasized his desire to reopen the country regardless of the consequences. He callously commented, "I'm not saying anything is perfect, and yes, will some people be affected, yes, will some people be affected badly—yes, but we have to get our country open, and we have to get it open soon." What more proof do you need that this man cares more about money than people? On one hand, you have Cuomo stating, "A human life is priceless." And on the other, you essentially have the president saying fuck the people. They can die as long as my economy doesn't suffer. But it gets better. (Seriously, if I were writing a novel, instead a non-fiction piece, this is about where I'd start to question if I went over the top in making Trump the villain. I can almost hear my writing friends saying, "But he can't be all bad. He needs some redeeming quality." Nope. Not in this case. There is no redeeming quality about him. Not in m opinion.) Trump went on to say, "I always felt 60, 65, 70, as horrible as that is. I mean, you're talking about filling up Yankee Stadium with death! So I thought it was horrible. But it's probably going to be somewhat higher than that." And he says it as if it's not a big deal, something we just have to accept.

Yet, here's the deal: those aren't abstract numbers. Each death was a person, a human being who had a family. My father wasn't just a statistic. He was my dad. He was the man my son couldn't wait to talk to every morning. The man who made my son laugh by making silly faces. There is a huge gaping hole in my life, in my mother's life, and in my son's life, and none of us give a shit about the economy at the moment. And I guarantee we are not the only Americans who feel this way. As I write, the death toll nears 72,000.

Yesterday, Governor Murphy said New Jersey schools will remain closed for the duration of the school year. That means my son, and hundreds of thousands of other New Jersey students, will finish out the year learning remotely. I've seen quite a bit of grumbling on social media about kids and parents who are annoyed there won't be a graduation or a prom this year. It sucks. It's unfortunate, but it could be worse. If you are only mourning the loss of one year of activities, you are relatively lucky. Think of all the families—the children and grandchildren and spouses—of someone who died; they are mourning the loss of an entire future of activities.

Murphy should probably just end the school year. While teachers are working harder than they ever have before, I'm not really sure students are learning. My son isn't. Remote activities—videos, games, educational websites—don't compare to being in school. They can't. What's the point of battling my child to get work done when I know that he will be no better off if he does it? Who are we trying to appease with this facade, this false idea that kids are being educated?

After my son completed his schoolwork, we went outside to play. I dug out our old badminton rackets and a shuttlecock that's older than he is. As he was tying his shoes, he looked up at me and smiled sadly. "I wish I could play with Grandpa." I know. I wish he could play with him, too.

Snapshot Rewind

2000: It was late July, and Mom and Dad were heading over to the bay beach in Peconic that we really like. I told them I'd join them later in the day. Since I wanted to go for a bike ride, I would bike over to the beach. They waited for me to get there to have lunch, and then we went swimming. When it started to get late, they left, and I told them I'd meet them at home in an hour. But I never made it. I hadn't even biked a half a mile when a woman rolled through a stop sign and smashed into me. She hit me hard enough that I flew off my bike and into the air. I crashed, headfirst, onto the hood of her car and then rolled off, my body smacking the road. I was wearing a helmet. If I hadn't been, I might have died or suffered brain damage because the helmet was cracked right down the middle. My entire body hurt. I couldn't even get up. Someone called 911, and an ambulance took me to the hospital in Greenport. I remember asking the cop who showed up to call my parents. Of course he didn't. He couldn't be bothered. He also lied on the police report, saying that I was biking on the wrong side of the road. If that was correct, I never would have been hit. It's simple logic. Either the cop wasn't terribly bright or he knew the woman who hit me and was trying to help her. Either way, it's proof that cops can't be trusted. Anyway, since the cop was too lazy to call my parents, they sat at home waiting for me. When I didn't arrive on time, they panicked. They knew something bad happened because I was always one of those kids who did as I said I would. Dad called the local hospitals. When he got through to the one in Greenport, they said someone matching my description had been brought in. He and Mom immediately got into the car and raced to the hospital to see if I was okay. It could have been worse. I could have died. But I had a broken thumb, a cracked sternum, and bruises all over my body. After a series of x-rays and other tests, the doctors finally let me leave. Mom and Dad took me home where they made me rest on the couch. We ended up having Chinese food for dinner and watching the movie *Angela's Ashes*. And that is how I paid for my first master's degree. With the settlement from the lawsuit, I was able to pay off my loans.

DAY 52

MAY 6, 2020

Last night, my son insisted on making chocolate ice cream sodas. Almost every night we spent here in the summers, Dad made them for us. But he's not here to make them anymore, so my son stepped into the role. Yesterday afternoon, when I was leaving to go grocery shopping, my son said, "Make sure you get milk, seltzer, and chocolate ice cream." He had already checked, there was still some chocolate syrup in the refrigerator from the last time Dad was there. After dinner, my son wouldn't let me help him make the sodas. "I used to watch Grandpa," he explained. "I know how to do it. It's my job now." And he did know how because it tasted just like Dad's.

Yesterday for dinner, I barbecued sausages for my son. As I stood at Dad's grill, a Manhattan in one hand and tongs in the other, smoke curling up from the meat, I thought of all the times Dad grilled when I was a kid. He'd bring out the meat on a plate and call over his shoulder, "Liz, get the gloves." While dinner cooked, he and I would play catch. Oh, the hours he and I spent playing catch.

The funeral home finally called to let Mom know she could pick up Dad's ashes. My brother drove her to get them, and the funeral home people handed Dad's ashes over in the parking lot. That really upset Mom. She couldn't go inside because of the pandemic—because everything is closed. But getting her husband's ashes in a parking lot seemed so cold, so impersonal, as if he were never a person at all. And now, it seems so final. The man I loved, the man who wiped away my tears countless times, the man who I didn't hug nearly long enough the last time I saw him, is now nothing more than a pile of ashes.

This afternoon, it was cloudy, damp, and chilly, but I suggested we go outside for a little while anyway. Fresh air is always good. But nothing I recommended—a walk, badminton, a trip to the beach—interested my son. While brainstorming ideas, he said, "I wish I had a kite." At which point I remembered that one summer—either last year or the year before—he got a kite as one of his summer reading prizes from the Mattituck library. Sure enough, when he looked in his dresser, he found one of those inexpensive kites. This one was designed to look like an American flag. The upper left-hand corner was blue with one big white star and a few smaller ones. The rest of the kite had red and white stripes. After taking it out, my son rummaged in his craft box for a black marker. He then proceeded to write, "Trump killed my grandpa, so dump Trump" on the kite. I chuckled. If Dad were here, he'd have smiled. That small political act would have made him proud.

Veteran's Beach was cold, but the wind did not disappoint. My son enjoyed flying the kite. Watching him, I thought of my dad. Daddy hated flying kites. He found it boring. But I still remember him taking me and my brother to that very same beach nearly forty years ago. It had been a cloudy day, too cool to go swimming, and so he brought us to the beach to fly kites. Being outside and doing something was always better than sitting inside and doing nothing, even if that something didn't excite Dad. He just wanted to make sure we were having fun. I also remember him flying a kite with my son—again at the same place we were today. My son was littler, and Dad patiently tried to help him get the kite aloft. Dad definitely mellowed as he got older. When it came to my son, he had more patience than he ever had with me as a child.

Snapshot Rewind

2013–2017: My son loved Treasure Beach, which is what he called the bay beach out in Peconic. I liked it, too. Sometimes when we went to that beach, Dad and I would strap the kayaks to the roof of the car. My son was too little to go out on his own, so he'd sit on my lap, and Dad and I would paddle our way through the inlet. Dad liked to go slow and enjoy the scenery. He'd take a few strokes and then hold the paddle up to his chest, parallel to the water, and simply drift. We liked Treasure Beach because the water in the channel was deep. We could dive in and the water would be over our head. I liked swimming across the channel. When my son was little, I'd push him across in his tube. As he got older and took swimming lessons, he would swim across with me. On the other side of the channel, the beach formed a peninsula, but my son called it an island. One day, he must have been about four, he got it into his head that pirates buried treasure on that beach, so he took his shovel, asked me to push him to the other side, and he started to dig. Obviously, he didn't find anything, but that gave us all an idea.

In the city, Mom went to a craft store. She bought three little wooden treasure boxes and some fake jewels. The next time we visited, she was prepared. While getting ready for the beach, I filled the boxes with the fake jewels, and Dad gave me some quarters. At the beach, we all swam across the channel. As Mom and Dad took my son in one direction to hunt for treasure, I set off in the opposite direction to bury the treasure. I marked each spot with a driftwood X. After signaling to my parents that I was done, they directed him over to where the treasure waited for him. The first time he dug out a treasure box, he squealed with delight. He believed he had found real pirate treasure. Each time we went to that beach, there was treasure to find, but as he got older, I had to employ more

232

and more stealth so that he didn't suspect I was the pirate. A couple of years ago, we stopped going to Treasure Beach. My son was disappointed, but the walk on the sand from the car to the beach was too far for Mom. Dad said her knees couldn't take the strain.

DAY 53

MAY 7, 2020

It's odd being in this house and being the adult. Being the parent instead of the child. Sure, I've been an adult for decades now, but whenever I came home, I still felt like a kid. Even when I brought my own child with me, Mom and Dad took care of the both of us. Dad went grocery shopping. Mom cooked dinner. But now that it's just me and my son, I'm the one taking care of him. Yes, I've been taking care of him for ten years, but being here is different. When I'm here, I'm used to being able to let go of responsibility. Life was carefree because Mom and Dad kept the world turning, and I was free to enjoy the moment.

This house is my son's art gallery. All around, especially on the mantel of the fireplace, are his pictures and crafts, gifts he made for my parents on their birthdays, on Mother's Day and Father's Day. Since this is where we usually saw my parents on those occasions, the gifts remain here as a reminder of a grandson's love for his grandparents. There are hedgehogs—three, to represent him, Nonna, and Grandpa—he made by cutting spheres of Styrofoam in half, sticking toothpicks into the body for quills, and adding googly eyes and some paint. There is a crab he made from a paper plate he painted red. It has hands—his hands traced and cut out—instead of claws. A picture of my son and Grandpa is framed with painted popsicle sticks and the words "#1Grandpa." One framed picture has two handprints—instead of flowers—attached to pipe cleaner stems stuck in a vase. A Teddy Roosevelt bear flies a kite with a key to represent Dad's two favorite historical Americans. A glass of wine and a hand pouring a bottle are painted on a board that was meant to be broken at Taekwondo. There are pictures of fish, sharks, and boats everywhere because even as a toddler, my son knew that Dad loved the water and all things associated with it.

I spoke to Mom this morning. She slept better last night than she had in a while. Having Dad's ashes put her more at ease. "He's home now," she said, and I couldn't quite share her relief. When I said I wanted Daddy to come home, that wasn't exactly what I had in mind. It's not what she wanted either. But at least she's no longer fretting that his body might somehow have gotten lost in the masses of dead that have filled New York City's morgues. I can't even imagine how awful this is for her. My parents were married for forty-eight years. None of us saw any reason to suspect they wouldn't easily make it to at least fifty. Since Dad retired, they were practically inseparable. They did everything together. And now, so unexpectedly, Mom is alone. Yes, she has her children and her grandchild, but it isn't the same. And once the pandemic ends, I won't be able to stay with her weekly in New York because my son will have to go back to school. I've suggested she move to New Jersey. That we look for a two-family house. But she isn't ready to move. She isn't ready to leave the house she lived in with Dad for forty-two years, the house in which they formed so many memories together. But she doesn't drive. And she doesn't walk well. How will she get around? How will she get groceries?

After lunch, my son and I went to Magic Fountain for ice cream. Dad didn't like the ice cream there, neither did Mom, but we went there often in the last several years because it made my son happy. We went there when I was a kid also—though it was probably under different management—but the real treat was when Dad took us into Greenport to get ice cream at Razzles. That place was awesome. Mom and Dad used to get butter pecan ice cream on sugar cones. My brother would order chocolate chocolate chip ice cream, also on a sugar cone, but I don't have a clue as to what I used to have. Why is that? Why can I remember everyone else, but not me? Maybe it's as simple as not being as predictable. Maybe I got something different each time. Back when I was still in high school, my cousin got married on Shelter Island. On the way home from the wedding, we stopped at Razzles. I think that was the last time we went. They have long since closed, and we have yet to find a place out here that is as good.

My son and I took our ice cream to the beach, and we sat on the sand by the water to eat it. When we finished, my son took Mom's metal detector to hunt for treasure, and we walked down the beach as far as we could, until the water pressed up against the bulkhead. Along the way, we passed the yacht club and the softball field where I used to play. Every summer during college, I joined the women's softball club out here. I played shortstop for the Fisherman's Rest team. It was fun, something to look forward to every week. Of course, Mom and Dad came to every game to cheer me on. The year we won the championship, one of my teammates had a party at her pool to celebrate. She even invited Mom and Dad to come because she felt as if they were part of the team.

Though we had an enjoyable walk, my son was disappointed not to find any treasure. All he uncovered was a rusty nail, a rusty knife blade, and a huge rectangular chuck of metal. No sign of Captain Kidd's treasure, nothing worth keeping. But being at the beach is better than being just about anywhere else during the lockdown. It is quiet, peaceful, and relatively empty. It felt like spring. There was only a slight breeze, and the water was calm. If only Dad was there, it would have been perfect.

For dinner, my son wanted a hamburger, but Daddy wasn't here to cook it, which meant the job fell to me. However, I never barbecued a hamburger—I avoid meat whenever possible—and I couldn't even call Dad to ask him how I should cook it. So I called my spouse. She laughed and gave me vague instructions, "Put the meat on the flame, cook it for a few minutes, then flip it." I asked what she meant by a few minutes, and she said, "When you think it might be ready." It seemed daunting, but I suppose the directions were good enough, or maybe Dad was somehow lending a spiritual hand because, according to my son, the burger came out good.

Snapshot Rewind
Circa 2014 and 2015: I taught my son how to read when he was three. My students in Korea had been two. I figured if I could teach them, why not teach my own son? I gave him a solid foundation in phonics and then taught him to read with flashcards and *Dick and Jane*. Very old school. But it worked. Far better, in my opinion, than some of these newer methods. After *Dick and Jane*, he graduated to the "Elephant and Piggie" books by Mo Willems. Oh, how he loved those books. And they were great because not only do they make reading fun, they also introduce kids to reading with emotion. One can't read "Elephant and Piggie" without varying the intonation in their voice. It just isn't possible. And no one read those books with more enthusiasm and excitement than Dad. Dad exaggerated every exclamation. No wonder my son enjoyed reading those books with his grandfather more than with anyone else. In the summer, he'd come out to the Mattituck house, and Mom and Dad would take him to the library. He'd grab a stack of the "Elephant and Piggie" books, and every night before bed, he and Dad would read together. Always, my son took Piggie's lines and Dad took Elephant's. Sometimes, my son would even act out Piggie's part—hopping or jumping on the bed.

One year for Dad's birthday—because they loved reading those books together—my son made Dad a picture of Elephant and Piggie. For Elephant's ears, he traced his hands— adding a bit of himself to the craft, as always. Above Elephant's head is a bubble that reads, "Piggie, what day is it?" The bubble above Piggie's head responds, "It is Grandpa's birthday." Daddy loved that picture. It might have been his favorite, because unlike the other works of art made by his grandson, he hung this one on his bedroom wall next to his bed. It's still there, and when I look at it, I can hear the two of them reading together.

DAY 54

MAY 8, 2020

Dad and I didn't always get along. There were things I did that angered him, and Dad's anger was never easy to endure. He had a temper that was quick to flare. And he was loud. When he yelled at me, I could feel my bones rattling inside my body. As a kid, I feared Dad's wrath, and maybe as I got older, I never lost that need to please him.

The summer before I started college, I totaled Dad's Buick. I asked him if I could borrow it to meet a friend at the movie theater in Greenport. He said yes, but then Mom realized she needed garlic for dinner. They told me I had to stop at the store first, get garlic, bring it home, and then I could go to the movies. I didn't have time to do it, so I drove faster than I should have, fast enough that when the road turned sharply to the left, the car continued to go straight and I flew head-first into a telephone pole. Dad was fuming mad. So mad that he told me I'd never be able to drive his car again. A punishment that lasted until he died. Only on two occasions did he temporarily lift the ban.

First, when Fireball developed a tumor on her heart. She needed to see a specialist, and Dad didn't want to take a day off of work if Mom and I could take her to the doctor. Needless to say, I was extremely nervous driving his car. But I got Fireball to and from the doctor safely. The second time was when Dad, Mom, and I went hiking and geocaching in Greenport. We wandered off the path in search of a cache, and then Mom's knees started to hurt. Sharp pain shot through her body making it difficult to walk,

There was no way she was going to make it back to where we parked, so Dad gave me the keys and told me get the car and "rescue" them.

Of course, Dad eventually got over his anger. Not enough to revoke the punishment, but enough to laugh about the incident. He often made sarcastic comments about sending me to the store to buy garlic. He waved to the "Elizabeth Pole" every time we passed it. And he eventually said, "That car gave me so much trouble. You really did me a favor." That was the last American-made car Dad ever bought. After that, he would only buy a Toyota. For years, he drove a Camry, but at some point, he switched to a RAV 4.

Then there was the time Dad—or maybe Mom—found a condom wrapper behind the couch in Mattituck. It wasn't mine. I will swear to that even now. But Dad didn't believe me. He was furious. It took my boyfriend at the time to come and talk to him for him to calm down. I'm not sure I ever saw him so angry. So, I suppose it's kind of ironic, in the end, that I had no interest in boys—and no use for condoms—at all.

After college, I went to Seoul, Korea, to teach English for a year. When my contract expired, I traveled for four months, which included seven weeks in India. While there, I got it into my head that I absolutely needed to get my nose pierced. I spent an entire day walking around Jaisalmer until I found a place that would do it. Weeks later, when I landed at Newark airport, I rushed through customs and immigration, excited to see my parents. Daddy immediately noticed the ring in my nose, and he was not pleased. I hadn't seen him in sixteen months, but when I went to hug him, he backed away. "What did you do to your nose?" He crossed his arms, fire in his eyes. He was that mad. Mad enough that he wouldn't hug me after a long absence. No, I'm not upset, not anymore. He eventually got used to the nose ring, even if he never learned to like it. And there were many hugs in the years that followed.

I hoped to go back to the beach or to a different beach today, but it rained earlier than the forecast had predicted, so after my son completed his schoolwork, he spent much of the day working on a jigsaw puzzle he found in Nonna's closet. Even when the rain stopped, it was cold and damp—not a beach day.

Snapshot Rewind

Summer 1979: Daddy snapped his Achilles tendon playing volleyball at a company picnic. The doctors were able to stitch the tendon back together. That time, his hospital stay was short. He was fixable, and he came home. But he had a cast on his leg that severely limited his mobility. For the rest of the summer, he didn't go to work. Since the injury happened at a company function, he was entitled to workman's comp. However, he couldn't drive, which meant we were stuck at home—no trips to the beach. No trips anywhere.

The cast came off just before Labor Day, and even though Dad wasn't supposed to drive, he couldn't resist the urge to go to the beach. After a summer stuck in the city, we all wanted and needed a day at the ocean, so Dad took us to Jones Beach. When we got there and set up the blanket, I was so excited, I couldn't wait to get into the water. I pulled off my shorts and shirt, and I didn't stop there. Caught up in my enthusiasm to get into the water, I tore off my bathing suit and ran naked down to the water. I was only four-years-old, but Dad was mortified.

DAY 55

MAY 9, 2020

It's sunny but cold, and the wind is fierce. When I woke up, it felt like winter. I hadn't brought a coat from home, but luckily, in the closet, I found one of Dad's to wear on my morning walk. Still, the wind sliced through me. As I read, the pages kept getting swept out of my fingers. I'm reading *The Blood of Olympus*, which is the final book in Rick Riordan's *Heroes of Olympus* series. It's not a book I ever would have picked up on my own, but my son loved the Percy Jackson books. I had once told him I'd read any book he wanted me to read so that we could talk about it. As he completed the Percy Jackson books, he handed them to me, and slowly, I found myself sucked into Jackson's world. My son and I had some great conversations regarding the characters and their adventures, and I was surprised by how much Greek mythology we both learned. Anyway, he blew through the Percy books but stalled halfway through the Heroes books. I, however, couldn't leave the series unfinished. And after reading *Pale Rider*, I needed something light, something fun, something that didn't require much thought. Mostly, I needed an escape into a world where the good guys always win. Where monsters are defeated and death is frequently defied.

I had to do laundry today, but there is no dryer. In Mattituck, we have to dry clothes the old-fashioned way by hanging them on a line. I only hope the wind doesn't steal them. My mother has always hung laundry outside—at both houses—even in the winter, when the cold cracks the skin on her hands.

While hanging laundry, my son asked me if he could have a Milky Way. In the freezer is a Ziplock bag full of fun-size Milky Ways. Every Halloween, my son went through his spoils, pulling out all the Milky Ways, and setting them aside for Dad. He knew they were Grandpa's favorite. When we came out to Mattituck in early November to rake leaves, he brought the candy. With a smile, he held them out to Dad, but he always had one caveat before handing them over, "You'll share them with me, right, Grandpa?" Of course he did, which is why they are still in the freezer. Dad was waiting for my son to visit so that they could eat them together. Now, my son will eat them alone.

My son and I went over to the sound to take a walk. The wind was sharp. I feared it might blow us into the water if we got too close. I'm not sure I've ever seen the sound as rough as it was this afternoon. Ocean-size waves crashed against the rocks, beat against the shore. Birds appeared to be flying backward as they battled their way through the wind. It's supposed to be spring, but the cold bit into my bones, making it feel like February. I wore Dad's jacket, and I had rummaged through Dad's hat box in search of a hat for my son. I found a woolen Looney Toons hunting cap. Under different circumstances, he might have grumbled that he was too old for a hat with a picture of Porky Pig and Daffy Duck. But it was Dad's, so my son wore it with a smile.

The wind stole two socks. Or a neighbor took them. When I brought in the laundry, I noticed two of my son's socks missing from the line—a pair. I find it too much of a coincidence that a pair would blow away together. Two random socks would be far more likely if it were an act of nature. What wind spirit intentionally seeks out matching socks?

I went outside to barbecue burgers again, and it was snowing. It's May—and it was *snowing!* As if this year hasn't been messed up enough. Normally, snow would make me happy. And all day, I've been looking forward to it, hoping it would hit us, but actually seeing it made me cry. It's one of those crazy quirks of life that I'd have loved to call Dad up to chat about.

A while ago, I wrote about Brian's father who was admitted into the hospital. He has COVID-19. At first, he had been showing signs of improvement. He had even been approved for the trial drug, Remdesivir. The family had been cautiously optimistic. But today, my friend messaged me to say that his dad's condition had gotten worse. The doctors said they could put him on a ventilator, but it would only keep his body alive. It would not save him. The family made the difficult decision to have him put in hospice in stead. Like my dad, he is not going to recover.

You know a disease is bad when it sweeps through an area, killing more than one person you know in less than a month's time. Brian had been in Boy Scouts with my brother years ago. Our Dads knew each other and the virus claimed both of them. Who would have thought all those years ago, when we watched the New York Giants win the Super Bowl, that one day a plague would settle over New York City and kill both of them? And I turn on the news, and I see people protesting because they don't want to wear masks, because they don't like being stuck at home, because they think the government is being oppressive. Well, this is the alternative: watching people you love die. And then reliving it when it happens to another family you know.

When my friend messaged me, I cried. I've been crying most of the day because I know exactly how it feels to have a parent die too soon. I'm crying for him. I'm crying for me. I'm still crying for my own Dad. But I also have to admit that I'm jealous. All Greek heroes had a fatal flaw, and when my son started reading the Rick Riordan books, he asked me what mine would have been. I have many flaws, but jealousy is probably my worst. I'm jealous tonight because as crappy as it is to have a parent die, Brian at least got to say goodbye—in person. He got to tell his father that he loved him one final time. I'm a terrible person for feeling like this. But it still hurts me so much that I didn't get one final hug. I didn't get to tell my father I loved him. I just hung up the phone, and that was it.

As I write, the death toll nears 80,000, and the rate of death doesn't show any sign of slowing down. States are opening up. People will continue to die because our federal government would rather dig graves than hand out more stimulus checks. Give your loved ones a hug. Tell them you love them. And never walk away angry.

Snapshot Rewind
Spring 1978: I didn't listen. And so it was my fault. I was three years old, and Daddy and I were roughhousing in the living room. After a while, Dad told me to stop, but I didn't. As he turned to sit up and reach for his glasses, I jumped over him. My foot hooked under his body, and I fell forward, smacking my left arm into the coffee table. The crunch of bone echoed through the room, and when Dad lifted my arm, it hung unnaturally in a U-shape. Both my radius and ulna snapped. Hearing the commotion, my mother ran into the room, and when she saw my arm, she burst into tears. They had to take me to the doctor, but they couldn't leave my infant brother home alone. In a panic, my mother called her parents—immigrants from Italy who spoke broken English. In the rushed conversation, partially in English and partially in Italian, something got lost in translation. My grandparents lived down the block and around the corner from us. Shortly after Mom hung up the phone, they arrived at our house frantic and breathless. Mom

245

pulled open the door, and my grandmother gasped, "What do you mean Elizabeth killed the baby?"

DAY 56

MAY 10, 2020

It's Mother's Day, though I suspect it is a sad and depressing day for many mothers this year. With stay-at-home orders in place, people will be traveling less and not visiting their moms. Restaurants are closed, so people who usually go out to eat will have to stay in. And with the recent deaths that have swept the country, the cloud of mourning will be hovering over many families. We are one of them. And while I woke up this morning, as I have for the last twenty-six days, missing Dad, I'm sure the day will be harder for Mom. This is the first Mother's Day in forty-five years that she will not have Dad to celebrate with her. Every year, at least in recent memory, he took her out to dinner. We couldn't always visit on Mother's Day. Sometimes we'd visit the weekend before or the weekend after, but Daddy was always there to take her out to dinner, to thank her for being a wonderful mother to his children. This year, I convinced my brother to be here for the day so that Mom would at least have her children and grandchild with her.

My son and I picked up bagels for breakfast and ate them at the beach before heading into the city to see Mom. The morning was cool but not nearly as windy as yesterday. When we got to Mom's, my son was excited to see his uncle's dogs, two Cavalier King Charles Spaniels. Petting and cuddling with them may have been the highlight of his day. My spouse drove in from New Jersey to spend the afternoon with us.

Dad's absence hung heavily around us. It was very disorienting being in the house on a holiday without him. But I suppose we had as pleasant a day as we could possibly have. Mom and I took a walk with the dogs. My son joined us for a little while, but he quickly got bored and ran back to the house to watch *Psycho*. For dinner, my brother cooked delicious Persian food. I especially liked the squash over rice with a pomegranate sauce. After we started eating, I realized no one initiated a toast. Daddy always toasted the moms on Mother's Day. So I raised my glass to Mom. "Happy Mother's Day."

But when my son raised his glass, he said, "A toast to Grandpa."

I smiled, and tears filled my eyes. "Yes. To Grandpa!" And we all clinked our glasses.

I am back in Long Island with my son. I didn't want to go back to New Jersey. I'm too unhappy in that condo, and with my son not physically attending school, there's no reason for me to be there. I asked my spouse to join us out here for the week so that we could all be together, but she'd rather be in New Jersey. She doesn't like it here. I don't like it there. I guess we need to find a different state to move to.

Tomorrow, my brother is taking Mom up to Cape Cod for a week. I'm glad she decided to go with him. Getting away for a while will probably be good for her. She needs to heal emotionally, and it might be easier in a place that's not saturated with memories of Dad.

Snapshot Rewind
2010: My son calls his favorite restaurant the Cherry Place. It's his favorite restaurant because the owner has always treated him like royalty when we go there for dinner. He calls it the Cherry Place

because once the owner found out how much he likes maraschino cherries, she started bringing him a glass full of them every time she brought us our drinks. Its real name, when it was on the water, was The Meeting House Creek Inn. It was tucked into the creek—a beautiful, idyllic place to sit, eat, and sip cocktails. Then they had to move and found a new location in downtown Riverhead where they rebranded themselves as the Pulaski Street Grill. My son's name for them never changed. Often, Mom or Dad would take us to dinner there, mostly because they treated my son well. When my son learned how to write script, he liked pretending that he was paying for dinner. Dad would hand over his credit card, but then my son—who shared his name—would sign the receipt. It made him feel important. Special.

The first time Dad took my son to the Cherry Place, he was four months old. It was my spouse's and my first Mother's Day as moms. My son was too little to eat restaurant food, but his smile and friendly disposition warmed the owner. At one point, she asked if she could hold him, and she carried him over to the bar where—with her holding him up—he wiggled his body and tapped his feet. Dad always enjoyed reminiscing about that first bar dance. When I think about it, I still hear Dad's laughter in my ear.

DAY 57

MAY 11, 2020

Brian's dad died yesterday, on Mother's Day. There were so many empty seats at dinner tables across the country, seats that should have been filled by people who were cut down by the virus.

I've spoken about Brian rather abstractly. Perhaps I should share some of our history, so that you can get to know him better. He and I were close in high school, but once I went off to college, I lost touch with everyone. However, years later we reconnected on Facebook. Back in high school, he was a writer. But when we friended each other on Facebook, I learned that somewhere along the way, he traded in his pencil for a camera. Now he is a talented photographer.

I've written about how I used to hate writing. That I found it oppressive and a waste of time—a tedious chore. It's Brian who changed that. One day, when I was a junior in high school, Brian suggested I keep a notebook and jot down stories or poetry, anything that struck me as interesting. I don't remember what my initial response was, but by my senior year, I had a pink spiral notebook in which I jotted my first pieces of creative writing. I still have the notebook. The writing is dreadful. But Brian planted the seed of how writing could be fun, a way to express my emotions, and slowly, over the years, I've cultivated my skill. I sometimes wonder if I ever would have found my way to writing if Brian had not suggested a notebook all those years ago. If he hadn't, perhaps you wouldn't be kicking back and reading my words now. Is it too late, after nearly thirty years, to say thank you?

And writing isn't the only skill I have to thank him for. One of my favorite memories of our friendship is the night he invited me to stay for dinner, and his parents ordered Chinese food. As he ripped open the bag and pulled out the food, he gave me a sly smile. With a glint in his eye, he said, "You can eat as much as you want, but you have to eat it with pencils." Then, he handed me a pair of chopsticks and proceeded to show me how to use them. I think of him every time I eat East Asian food.

As I've mentioned, I knew him through the Boy Scouts. His Dad, my dad, and another father were quite close—"The Three Musketeers." Not only did they joke around and have fun on Boy Scout outings, they also did things together outside of the Boy Scouts. They and their spouses went to dances and dinners. We went to barbecues and other events. But then something happened around the time I left for college. I'm not sure what. Dad never really seemed to know either, but he had fallen from the fold and no longer hung out with the other families. It made him sad, and he often looked back on the good times they shared rather wistfully, wishing the friendships had continued.

Boy Scouts was my brother's thing. It's really his story to tell, but I am the sentimental one. The storyteller. The one who feels compelled to write about Dad. And Dad's story would be incomplete without at least a blurb or two dedicated to the Scouts, since he really valued the time he got to spend with my brother. Every month the Scouts went camping. If Dad didn't go on every camping trip, he went on some of them, and he hated it, or so he said. I remember him coming home from camping trips smelling like a campfire and complaining about the cold, the rain, and the miserable sleeping conditions—the loud snores that kept him awake. However, as he got older, he spoke more fondly, more nostalgically about the trips. I'm not sure if time had allowed him to romanticize his experiences or if he just exaggerated his discontent in the moment because it made for a better story. Either way, I know he didn't enjoy camping for the sake of sleeping in the woods. He did it because he felt it was a way to connect with my brother.

Despite his lack of enthusiasm for camping, there were two campsites that Dad really liked. His favorite was Treasure Island— I think that's what it was called, but obviously, I can't call him up to confirm it. It was on an island in the Delaware River, and other than Dad saying everyone had a fantastic time there, I don't remember the specifics of why he liked it.

He also very much enjoyed Baiting Hollow, which is on Long Island, about a twenty minute drive west of the Mattituck House. After my son's Tiger year (first year) of Cub Scouts, we sent him to a day camp in Watchung Reservation, not too far from where we live. Other Scout parents had raved about it, and so we thought it might be fun for our son. He liked it, but he didn't love it. When he spoke about it, his voice was void of enthusiasm. But during his Wolf year (second year), he asked if he could go back. I liked the idea of summer camp, but I wanted something better. Something with a lake, a more traditional type of camp. The kind you see on television and in the movies. I set out to do some research. There were other camps in Jersey, but they were all an hour or more away, and in rush hour traffic, driving was not an appealing option. Then, I remembered Baiting Hollow, and how Dad raved about it all those years ago. I googled the camp, and sure enough, they had a summer program for Cub Scouts.

That spring, when we went out to Mattituck for Easter, I told Dad that I was thinking about sending my son to camp at Baiting Hollow. Dad was oh so very excited. Not only did he insist on paying for it—yet another gift for his grandson—he had us all pile into the car, and we drove down to the campground. He wanted his grandson to see it, and his enthusiasm was infectious. When we arrived, we met one of the Scoutmasters who ran the camp. He was the only one there, but he, too, got caught up in Dad's excitement, and he took us on a tour. As he showed us around, Dad reminisced about being there with my brother. It's as if he had momentarily traveled back in time, revisiting moments that brought him a great deal of pleasure.

Since the camp was too far away for me to attend the parent orientation in June, my parents went in my place. I think Dad actually enjoyed going—another trip down memory lane. When they asked who his child was, and he told them, the woman running the orientation asked, "But if he lives in Jersey, how will he get here every day?"

Dad, being Dad, responded, "You mean there isn't a bus?" It took the woman a moment to realize Dad was joking, but when she did, she laughed. Dad explained that while his grandson lived in New Jersey, he'd be staying in Long Island during the week of camp.

Two weeks later, my son insisted that Dad take him to his first day of camp, so the three of us went. I'm not sure who was more excited—Dad, or my son.

Of course, Dad also came with me to pick up my son—or rather I went with Dad, since he drove. The minute my son saw us, he came sprinting toward us waving his arm—which sported a blue bracelet. "I passed," he said. "I passed my swimming test." That meant he got to swim in the deep end.

Dad hugged him. "Congratulations! That's great." Dad then told us about when he spent a week during the summer with my brother at Yawgoog Scout Camp in Rhode Island. They also had to take swimming tests. Even all those years later, Dad was still proud of the fact that he and my brother had both passed. "We were the only ones in the troop," he said with a smile.

My son enjoyed camp so much that he asked if he could please go to the sleep-away camp the following year. Of course, my spouse and I said yes, and once again, Dad insisted on paying for it. When I tried to object, he said, "But I want to do this. Please, let me do it for him."

Sleep-away camp proved to be even more fun than day camp. When we picked up my son at the end of his stay, he asked me if I would please buy him the pocket knife that he really liked—one with wolves on the handle—in the gift shop. Before I could answer, Dad pulled out his wallet, although he did ask me if it was okay before he handed over the cash. In the car, the two of them were already talking about next year. Dad promised to send him to camp again since he had so much fun. None of us had a clue that Dad would not live to see another summer.

Now, my son is searching for every possible way to hold on to his grandfather. I think that's why he wants to play baseball. Yesterday, when we were in Queens, he unearthed my first baseball glove. He decided he needed to keep it—despite having his own glove at home—so he brought it to Long Island. After completing his schoolwork today, he wanted to play catch. Great idea, except my glove is also at home. But I did a little rummaging and found Dad's glove. The glove he had as a kid, the glove he spent countless hours wearing when we played catch together. The leather is torn and cracked, but the webbing is intact, and the pocket is well formed.

I smiled as I slipped my hand into it and went out to play with my son.

Snapshot Rewind

1989: Dad was a jokester. He liked to laugh and have fun. My brother's Scoutmaster was strict. His rules were gospel, and he didn't take kindly to people flouting them. His name was Mr. Bley, though Dad often referred to him as Captain Bligh, a reference to the British Naval officer most famously known for the mutiny that occurred aboard his ship, the *HMS Bounty*. One year, for the father and son spring trip, the Scouts went to Hershey Park in Pennsylvania. On the bus, Dad and his two friends—"The Three Musketeers"—passed the time singing. The noise irked the Scoutmaster. He told them to be quiet. They sang louder. To silence them, he threw a block of wood at them. They increased the volume further. By the time they reached the park, the Scoutmaster was boiling with frustration. He reprimanded them. In response, to provoke him further, they posed as the three wise monkeys. My Dad covered his eyes, Brian's dad covered his ears, and the third father covered his mouth—see no evil, hear no evil, speak no evil. Yes, they definitely shared some good times and had some happy memories. I guess that's what life is about: enjoying moments when you can and collecting stories to look back on, stories that still, after decades have passed, make you smile.

DAY 58

MAY 12, 2020

Dad died four weeks ago. Damn! Four weeks without Dad. And the days will only stretch out further with me missing him more. As states begin to relax restrictions and Trump pushes America to open up, Dr. Fauci—the one sane voice of reason on the Corona- virus Task Force—is going to testify today before the Senate to warn that opening too quickly will lead to more suffering and death. I seriously don't understand why anyone would choose money over life. Cash over love. Maybe they are incapable of love. Or they think this can't happen to them, or anyone they care about. The Republican Party has labeled itself the Christian party, the moral party, the pro-life party. Well, it's hard to think of them as pro-life anymore, not when the leader of their party is responsible for 82,000 American deaths. A new projection has the death toll rising to 147,000 by early August—that's up 10,000 from yester- day. I don't think the Republican Party should continue branding themselves as Christian *and* capitalistic. If nothing else, the crisis arising from this pandemic is demonstrating that Christian values, genuine Christian values, are not comparable with capitalistic ones. You can't exploit people and protect them at the same time.

For school, my son had to write another poem. I haven't been able to get him to write any prose since Dad got sick, but he appears to be using poetry as a way to process his grief:

The Door

There was a door
on the second floor
covered in dust
and rust.
It had a hole
big enough for a soul,
but on the other side
you would need a guide
to get out
without a shout.

My spouse and I decided that, if school does not resume in-person classes come September, I will homeschool our son. It was the plan for this year. We even had the principal send us the withdrawal forms. But they arrived in my inbox the same day Dad got sick. With Dad dying, I just didn't have the headspace to be a full-time teacher. Some days, I still feel like I'm in a fog.

Some days, I'm not sure I can be a good parent without Dad around to offer me advice. Though, when I didn't listen to him, I guess things still turned out okay—like with the balance bike. I first learned about their existence when my son was in a stroller. I was taking him for a walk in the park and I saw a kid on one. Shaking my head at the oddity of it, I asked his mother where the pedals were. She laughed, explaining that balance bikes were a new fad out of Europe. The hardest part of learning to ride a bike is the balance. So the idea was to teach kids balance before teaching them how to pedal. I was intrigued, so much so that for Christmas—the week before my son turned three—my spouse and I gave him a balance bike. Dad ridiculed me, calling me a snob because I thought something European might be better than something

American. But I didn't let him deter me. By October, my son was riding a two-wheeler. And the fact that his grandson could ride a bike before he turned four impressed Dad enough that he finally conceded. "It was a good idea. You did good. I'm glad you didn't listen to me."

Snapshot Rewind

Late 1970s: Daddy always loved the water. Before my parents rented or bought the house in Long Island, we spent many summer days at Jones Beach. Sometimes we'd go early and spend all day. Sometimes we'd leave the house a little later. Mom would make lemon chicken for dinner, pack it up for a picnic, and we'd stay at the beach long after most other people had left. The beach in the evening, after the crowds dissipated, was always the most enjoyable time to be there. It's been years since I've eaten Mom's lemon chicken. It might even be years since she made it. But sometimes when I'm at the ocean with my family, after the lifeguards have packed up and the sun hangs low in the sky, I swear there are moments when I can smell the lemony scent of it in the air.

DAY 59

MAY 13, 2020

In May of 2017, after more than 100 years, The Ringling Brothers and Barnum and Bailey Circus closed. I was visiting my parents in February of that year when we heard on the news that the circus would be coming to an end. Dad didn't hesitate. He immediately went online to book tickets for all of us—my son, my spouse, me, Mom, and himself—to go. The circus was too big of a deal to miss. An era was drawing to a close, and Dad wanted to make sure that his grandson got to experience it before it was no more. We had a fantastic day. Mom and Dad bought us all clown noses to wear. And of course, Dad bought my son the souvenir of his choice—a plastic sword that cost way more than it was worth. It was a fun afternoon. My son started the day in a bad mood, but the excitement of the tigers, the clowns, and acrobats eventually captivated him and cheered him up. He was always happy to spend a day with his grandfather. After the circus, Dad took us out for ice cream at Eddie's Sweet Shop, our favorite ice cream place in Queens.

The lawn needed to be mowed. Dad always did it. Now, the duty falls to me. For the first time ever, I used a lawn mower. Living in a condo, yard work isn't necessary, and Dad never wanted me to do it here. Raking leaves, yes. Mowing the lawn, no. I've no idea why. The hardest part was the noise. I don't do well with motors—the noise causes me physical pain—but I managed to get through it by stopping frequently. My son came out to help. He was excited to use the mower. But he pushed it back and forth about three times, and he was done. The novelty quickly wore off, and television was more fun.

Two falls ago, when I came out here to rake leaves for Dad, I signed my son up for a half a day shooting event at Baiting Hollow Scout Camp. My son loves the shooting activities—BB guns and archery—so I thought it would be a fun activity for him. I told Dad to go with my son. Every year, I do many scouting activities with him. I thought he would enjoy being with his grandfather for a change. After all, he always liked saying, "The boys with the boys," when he was with Grandpa. Dad wanted me to go, too, but there were lots of leaves to pick up. It was, after all, the reason I had gone out to Mattituck to begin with. Besides, two adults would have been too much. I didn't want my son to feel smothered. As I expected, Dad had a great time. He enjoyed watching his grandson shoot. And my son was thrilled to spend the day with Grandpa.

My son, who hates Zoom calls and the whole concept of talking to any adult—not including moms or grandparents—via video chat, asked me if he could please FaceTime with my friend, Bonnie, in Washington. I was shocked, but when I told Bonnie that he wanted to speak with her, she was happy to talk to him. This evening, she called after she finished with work. As expected, my son was shy at first. He wanted me to sit with him and point the camera only on me. But he warmed up and was soon running around with my phone, showing my friend various things in the house, including the 1,000-piece puzzle he's been working on. As he eased into the conversation, he was laughing and joking around. When we got off the phone, he said, "I really like her. I can't wait to visit." Because when the pandemic ends, my son will need a healing trip, an escape from the horrors of the last two months. And my friend has invited us to come stay with her once it's safe to travel again.

Snapshot Rewind

1991: My brother once told Mom and Dad that they weren't good parents because they never got him a dog. The guilt must have worked because when he graduated middle school, they bought him a puppy. My brother named her—a purebred golden retriever—Lady Fireball Excalibur, but we all called her Fireball. When we brought her home, Dad laid down the rules. He intended to be strict. "Under no circumstances," he told us, "will she ever be allowed in my bed." I have no idea if he was serious or if he actually intended to follow through with the rules. Generally, Dad didn't bend once he issued a proclamation.

However, a few weeks later, it was time to take her for a walk, and I couldn't find her. (Yes, she was my brother's dog, but ultimately, I'm the one who took her for walks, and years later, I'd be the one who would be called on to take care of her when my parents were away. I didn't mind. I loved her, too.) I looked through the entire house, and she was nowhere. Then, I walked into Dad's bedroom, and there she was. Dad was on the bed watching some sporting event on television, and cuddled next to him was Fireball. So much for the rules. Apparently, when it came to Fireball, they no longer applied.

DAY 60

MAY 14, 2020

Mom and Dad got married on September 18, 1971. Their wedding song was "We've Only Just Begun" by the Carpenters. I was born three years later, on September 11. (My birthday is now a national day of mourning. Remember when the deaths of 3,000 Americans in one day was cause for anger and outrage? We went to war over it. But I guess it's only a problem for middle America when the deaths are caused by Muslim terrorists. When our own president shrugs off the deaths of 3,000 Americans in one day—times many days—and claims it's the price to pay in order to rescue our economy, his supporters applaud him. They embrace the death of our elderly as a way to "Make America Great Again.") And I came home from the hospital on their anniversary. As a kid, I always joked that I was their best anniversary present. Now, as a mom, I realize I was probably right.

Last September, things were—mentally and emotionally—bad for me. The last thing I wanted was to start another school year living in my condo. It is a toxic environment that exacerbates everything else that feels wrong in my life. My mental state was crumbling. I was depressed and anxious and miserable. The morning of my birthday, I felt even worse. Another year older, and nothing to show for it. I wasn't anywhere near where I had once hoped to be at that point in my life. A series of dead ends and failures had me feeling completely hopeless. That morning, when my parents called to wish me a happy birthday and to FaceTime with my son, they could hear the anguish in my voice. It worried them.

They got into the car, and Dad drove to New Jersey to surprise me. The moment Dad walked through the door and pulled me into a hug, I felt as if I had been pulled from a lake after treading water for hours. Just having him there made everything better. He told me to pick a place for lunch and he would take me out. But I said we had to pick up my son first. If he knew his grandparents had visited and he didn't get to see them, he would be angry. I don't think Dad expected me to pull him out of school, but the moment I suggested it, his eyes lit up, and he smiled. "Okay, let's do it." We went to a hibachi restaurant in Somerville. The food was good. The company even better. We laughed together and ate way too much. By the time Mom and Dad brought me back home, I was smiling.

Daddy died a month ago. I still cry every day. Sometimes I wake up crying because the pain of missing him is great. Since he died, thousands more have joined him. As of today, 86,000 Americans have died from the virus, but medical experts think the numbers are even higher. Of course, you have the Trump supporters and people pissed off about being stuck at home who are claiming the death toll is actually much lower. In Wisconsin, the State Supreme Court overturned the Democratic governor's stay-at-home order, declaring that it was unlawful. Republicans in the legislature filed the lawsuit, claiming that the stay-at-home order would be bad for business. Companies would suffer. People would lose their jobs. What will they say when people start dying?

You also have Republicans pushing for schools to open up in the fall. Rand Paul claims that the mortality rate among kids is so low that it would be foolish to keep schools closed. What about teachers? Some of them are in the vulnerable age group. Asymptomatic kids can infect other family members. But what concerns me most is the fact that kids are now falling ill from a COVID-related inflammatory illness. While most cases, not surprisingly, are in New

York, seventeen states have reported sick children. Three children in New York have died. I'm having a hard enough time processing Dad's untimely death. I can't fathom what the parents of those children are going through.

As my son and I kicked back on the beach this afternoon, eyes closed, listening to the rhythmic rippling of the water, I realized that I won't be able to move forward unless I let go of the things that I can't control. I need to let go of Mom's pain and my son's sorrow. Trying to absorb it isn't helping them. It's wearing me down and making it more difficult to support them in other ways. My own pain is heavy enough. I need to let go of regret. I will never have that final morning with Dad back again. I can't go back and give him one last hug. I can only hope that in the end he knew I loved him. I also need to let go of all my future plans with Dad. My wishes and expectations for things we'd do and places we'd go. Holding onto them, thinking continuously of all the things he will miss, won't help me. Thinking of the things he wanted to be present for, the things he wanted to be able to do for my son, won't bring him back. It will only make living without him harder. I need to let go of the what-ifs. They don't matter anymore. Replaying them only makes me sadder.

What I won't let go of is my anger at Trump and the federal government for their failed response to this pandemic. A strong, solid, moral leader would not have been able to avert every death, but he or she wouldn't have ignored the intel. A good leader would have acted quickly and decisively. A compassionate leader might have saved Dad. A responsible president wouldn't have fed the American people a stream of continues lies. And an ethical president would have put lives before money. I won't let go of my anger because there is a lesson to be learned, one to pass on to my son. Being politically conscious and aware is important. When a nation follows a false god, people die. It has happened before. It will happen again.

I also won't let go of the memories. The good times I had with Dad. The special moments he and my son shared. These I will hold onto tightly, and maybe, someday, I can remember them without tears.

Tonight, when my son was once again making chocolate ice cream sodas, I offered to help. He looked at me sideways with a lopsided smile and said, "I am the sole heir of Grandpa's ice cream sodas. No one is allowed to make them but me."

Snapshot Rewind
May 14, 2005: Today is the fifteenth anniversary of my wedding reception. Yes, my wedding and my reception did not occur on the same day. Fifteen years ago, we weren't legally permitted to get married in our own country, so we had to travel to Canada. However, my spouse wanted a traditional reception, so we celebrated the month after we got married. Usually, the bride dances with her father and the groom his mother. Since we were both brides, we thought it would be silly to have two daddy-daughter dances, which meant we had to agree on one song. My spouse and I rarely agree on anything. I didn't like any of the songs she picked. She didn't care for the one I liked, but to avoid a standstill, she gave in. We danced with our fathers to Bette Midler singing "The Wind Beneath My Wings."

Since we didn't have a wedding party—a best man—I asked Dad if he would give the toast. He was happy to do so. Mom said he worked hard on the speech wanting to get it just right. I wish I had saved his speech the way I had saved his notes when he came up to school to talk to my son's class. But I didn't. Anyway, when he held up his glass to toast me and my spouse, I was happy. We were all smiling. The world seemed perfect.

EPILOGUE

JUNE 2021

On Day 5, I wrote, "I have no idea what will greet us at the other end of this pandemic. Life won't be the same. I may or may not have a job. I may or may not be able to move. I may or may not get a break with my writing. But I'll have my family—hopefully—and I'll have my wine. I'll take it!" As you know, I don't have my family. Not everyone. This pandemic stole my father. It fractured my family.

Not wanting to send our child to school in the midst of a pandemic, my spouse and I decided to homeschool him. He hated getting on camera, and while the virtual model was great for keeping people safe, it was not as effective as in-person learning. So, we scrapped "real school" for the year, and I immersed my son in a rigorous humanities program. We spent most of the first semester living in Mattituck—just the two of us, removed from the rest of the world. It was blissful. If Dad had survived, it might have been perfect. Around Christmas, we returned to New Jersey so that we could pack and finally move out of the condo.

Being a full-time teacher for my son left me little time to do much else. I couldn't earn a living—not that anyone was hiring anyway. By the time my son went to bed at night, I was tired, but I attempted to keep writing. I tried to revise my unpublished novel about a genderqueer teen who is suicidal due to her mother's intense Christian beliefs, but I ended up getting frustrated by the fact that it didn't seem to be going anywhere. After eight months, I filed it away in a digital folder. Maybe someday, I'll return to it. However, I did complete several essays—all of them about Dad. About missing him. Literary magazines, both online and print, published a few of them. Minor successes.

In the early days of my blog, I wrote favorably about Governor Cuomo. While I still believe he acted very much like a leader should, scandals have tarnished his reputation. But by now they have been rehashed so frequently in the news, it would be redundant to write further about them here. Also, I should note Trump lost his bid for reelection. People came out in record numbers to vote for Biden. The message was clear. Americans had had enough of Trump's lies, his inhumanity, his stupidity. (Sadly, though, memories are short. Four years later, in 2024, Trump was reelected.)

My friend Brian, in an attempt to grapple with his father's death, turned to advocacy. He worked tirelessly with various organizations to ensure that the victims of COVID will be remembered.

Mom finally sold Dad's car on Labor Day weekend 2020. While we were busy inside dealing with the car salesman, my son went missing. I found him in the lot, sitting in the driver's seat of Dad's car, his hand on the steering wheel and an intense look of sorrow etched on his face. The following year, Mom sold the Mattituck house. She doesn't drive and couldn't get out there without me. I would have loved to have gone there more frequently, but once the world opened up, it wasn't possible. I still cry when I think about it. I had thirty years of memories tied up in those walls. It was my happy place, the one place in the world I always felt safe, and now, it is gone. My son also misses it.

In February 2021, after a twenty-five-year journey, I finally earned my black belt in Taekwondo. It was a bittersweet moment. Of course I was ecstatic to have attained my goal, but it was my first achievement in a world without Dad. I so desperately wanted him to be there watching me test. I wanted so badly to call him up and tell him that I did it. Instead, I cried because he couldn't be there, because I will never again hear him say, "Very nice" when I accomplish something.

I wonder often, did anyone else on that Viking cruise get sick? Did anyone else die? We only hear about the cases on the cruises that captured media attention. But what about the cruise that killed my father? I wanted to hold them responsible. A healthy man goes on vacation and comes home infected with a deadly virus. That's not acceptable. What did the staff know that they refused to share with the passengers? My guess is that somewhere along the line, they started hiding the truth. I wanted my mother to sue them, but the entire process seemed too daunting, so she opted not to follow through.

On April 14, the one-year anniversary of Dad's death, we finally had a funeral/memorial Mass for him. My son and I both wrote a eulogy. He did a better job delivering his. I sobbed throughout my entire reading.

A few weeks after the memorial Mass, I got my first tattoo. Missing Dad saying, "Very nice," I had the words—in his handwriting—tattooed on my left inner wrist.

At the time of writing this epilogue, COVID has killed 618,258 Americans. The world is beginning to open up, and people are talking about a return to normalcy. But let me be completely clear. For me and the families of those who died, life will never return to normal. We will never be able to reclaim our pre-COVID lives. My Dad was such a big part of my life and my son's life that we are still trying to find our way in a world without him. If there was anything even close to normal in our lives right now, we'd be getting ready to spend the weekend with him for Father's Day.

But he is gone forever, so I will leave you with one final story.

It took six months, but my son finally returned to Taekwondo via Zoom. And when in-person classes resumed with low-capacity limits, he excitedly started attending class again. He even participated in several virtual tournaments.

In February 2020, my son competed in a tournament out in Pennsylvania. Mom and Dad were getting ready for their cruise through Patagonia, and they didn't want to go to a crowded venue that might be crawling with germs. Dad didn't want to get sick before he left because that might have ruined his trip. (He had no idea that there would be worse germs on the boat, germs that would not only ruin his trip but end his life.) Anyway, the day of the tournament, Dad texted my son on his tablet, "Good luck pal. I'll be with you in spirit." None of us had a clue how foreshadowing those words would be.

Less than a month later, the world shut down, and the rest of the tournament season was canceled. As a result, the 2020 District Tournaments were postponed until June 2021. To compete in districts, you need to qualify, and my son did so in three events: traditional forms, weapons, and sparring.

The Northeast District Tournament was held in Lancaster, Pennsylvania. In the morning, the day of the event, the boys in my son's ring gathered on the mat, and I started to feel increasingly worried. Nervous. So many of the competitors wore uniforms that said "State Champion" or "District Champion" on their backs. The competition would be fierce, the toughest my son had ever faced. My fear was that he wouldn't do well and that a finish toward the bottom of the pack would discourage him. It's not that I didn't think he was good. But seeing so many champions made me wonder if they might all be better. I should have had more faith in my son.

Even though my son said he was nervous, he looked completely calm on the mat. For traditional forms, the judges called him to perform second. There was a time he didn't do all that well if he was in the first three to perform. The way it works is three competitors do their form, and then the judges call the three of them up to give their scores one at a time. After that, each person gets their score immediately after they perform. The forms look much like a dance—rhythmic and graceful. But if you watch closely, you can also see how deadly some of those moves could be if used in a fight. Overall, my son's form looked crisp and strong, perhaps one of his best performances. When the first three boys were given their scores, my son and the boy who went after him tied. I began to hope that my son might actually place. Throughout the course of the competition, only one boy scored better. At the end, there was a three-way tie for second. The three boys had to do their form again. I was terribly nervous. But my son did amazing, and the judges agreed. He ended up in second place.

In weapons, my son also did well. Usually the kids who do nunchucks or the staff score highest. But my son placed second with the oh-sung-do—the one-handed sword. Two medals—not bad. As for sparring, he lost the first round, but while he's been working hard on his forms this year, he hasn't sparred much. The pandemic hasn't allowed it.

There is no doubt; Dad was definitely with my son in spirit. Which gives me hope that maybe he is still with me as well.

RECIPES

Food was important to Dad. It was a way to spoil his family, especially his grandson. Throughout my memoir, I wrote about Dad's connection to certain foods and my memories of them. So that you may remember my dad and our story, I want to leave you with a few of his favorite recipes.

WAFFLES

The imprecise measurements are part of the charm.

- 2 cups flour
- Less than 1 teaspoon of salt
- 1 good teaspoon of baking powder
- 1 heaping teaspoon of sugar
- A little less than 3 cups milk
- 2 or 3 eggs
- 5 tablespoons melted sweet butter

1. Mix dry ingredients together. Add milk to dry ingredients one cup at a time. Mix with a whisk between cups. Add butter. Whisk until the batter is smooth. Pour batter into waffle iron (and follow waffle iron directions).

CHOCOLATE ICE CREAM SODA

1. In a tall glass add about an inch and a half of U-Bet chocolate sauce.

2. Add roughly ¼ cup milk. Whole milk works best. Stir until milk is chocolatey.

3. Add cold seltzer, letting it get frothy on top. Stir.

Add a large scoop of chocolate ice cream. Dad's preference was s Häagen-Dazs.

CRUMB CAKE

Cake Batter:

- 1 ½ cups flour
- ½ cup sugar
- ¾ cup milk
- 1 egg
- ½ teaspoon salt
- 1 teaspoon vanilla extract
- 3 teaspoons baking powder
- 2 tablespoons softened butter

Crumb Topping:

- 1 pound frozen butter

- 4 cups flour

- 1 ½ cups sugar

- 2 tablespoons cinnamon

- ½ teaspoon salt

- Powdered sugar for top of cake

1. Preheat oven to 350 degrees. Grease and flour a large (11x15) jelly roll pan.

2. Cream together sugar and butter. Add egg. Add milk and vanilla. Stir in flour, salt, and baking powder. When the batter is smooth, pour into the pan and spread evenly.

3. For the crumb topping: Add flour, sugar, cinnamon, and salt in a large mixing bowl. Cut frozen butter into small cubes. Using your hands, squeeze butter into dry ingredients. Sprinkle crumbs over cake batter.

4. Bake at 350 degrees for 30 minutes.

5. When cake cools, sift a generous amount of powdered sugar on top of crumbs.

ACKNOWLEDGEMENTS

A decade ago, my friend, Bonnie, gifted me a tarot reading with a friend of hers, Nancy Lukas. The cards foretold that above all else I needed to keep writing. At the time, I wrote mostly fiction, though I had yet to publish anything. The cards, however, saw me shifting my focus to non-fiction. I wish I could remember Nancy's exact words, but the best I can do is paraphrase. She essentially told me: *Someday you will experience something painful, but writing about it will help others. It will also be your breakthrough work.* I spent years speculating what that something might be, but never did the possibility of a worldwide pandemic that would kill my father ever cross my mind. That tarot reading, on many occasions, gave me hope—when I was feeling nothing but despair—that someday I would be successful. I would publish a book. I just had no idea that when victory came, it would be bittersweet. I wish more than anything, that my dad had survived to see my success, but it's his story—his life—that brought me here. I know he would be proud.

I want to thank Summer for giving new life to my Pandemic Memorial to my father. The editorial staff at Unsolicited Press has been wonderful and I truly appreciate all of you. I also want to thank Bill Mesce who, when I asked him for help, not only said "yes," but followed through. For that, I will always be grateful.

Louise Stahl has endured hearing my ups and downs in the writing world more than anyone else, and she has been a constant voice telling me not to give up. When I told her I wanted to turn my Pandemic Diaries blog into a manuscript, she quickly volunteered to help. For her support and patience in reading and rereading and editing the most depressing thing I've ever written, thank you.

I also could not have reached this point of seeing one of my manuscripts in print without the emotional and writing support

I've gotten from Jin Cordaro and Lauren Guastella. Thank you for pushing me and trying to keep me positive. And thank you to Diana Olsen who convinced me to go back to writing when I tried so hard to quit. Persistence is key.

In the early days of my grief, Clare Morris, then editor at the *Blue Nib*, accepted and published essays about Dad and learning to navigate the world without him. They were much needed glimmers of happiness in a sea of sorrow. Thank you, Clare, for reminding me that good exists even in the midst of bad, and for providing another outlet for my work.

Thank you to my son, Gary III, for being my constant muse. I've probably written more since he was born than I ever did before. Thank you Kati Jaeger for picking up the domestic slack during 2020 when I was just trying to survive day to day. And thank you for reviewing my exponential growth numbers.

Thank you to all my early readers—Kerry, Anna, Tani, Marguerite, Veronica, Donna, Dale, Brian, Janet, and Dennis.

A special thank you—and Merry Christmas!—to Bonnie Betts. Despite living on the opposite side of the country, she walked with me through the darkest days of the Pandemic. I don't know how I'd have pulled through without her constant calls, gifts, messages, encouragement, and support. Pain is definitely easier to endure when it is shared.

And finally, thanks Mom for always being there and Dad for giving me enough happy memories to write a book.

ABOUT THE AUTHOR

Stolen: Love and Loss in the Time of COVID-19 is Elizabeth Jaeger's first book. Her essays, short stories, book reviews, and poetry have been published in various print and online journals, including *Margate Bookie, Caustic Frolic, The Blue Nib, Capsule Stories, Watchung Review, Ovunque Siamo,* and *Italian Americana. Newtown Literary* published "The Treehouse," which is a chapter from her novel in progress. Jaeger earned an MFA in creative writing from Fairleigh Dickinson University and an MA in history from William Paterson University. Currently, she teaches history at Perth Amboy High School. She lives in New Jersey with her wife, son, and three cats, though she is always happiest when traveling and exploring new places.

You can find her at: www.elizabethjaegerauthor.com and on Tik-Tok @PapaJaegerTheOwl

ABOUT THE PRESS

Unsolicited Press is based out of Portland, Oregon and focuses on the works of the unsung and underrepresented. As a womxn–owned, all–volunteer small publisher that doesn't worry about profits as much as championing exceptional literature, we have the privilege of partnering with authors skirting the fringes of the lit world. We've worked with emerging and award–winning authors such as Shann Ray, Amy Shimshon–Santo, Brook Bhagat, Kris Amos, and John W. Bateman.

Learn more at Unsolicitedpress.com. Find us on Twitter and Instagram at @UnsolicitedP.

www.ingramcontent.com/pod-product-compliance
Lightning Source LLC
Chambersburg PA
CBHW030409130626
46549CB00004B/1687